DIVING
BRITISH VIRGIN ISLANDS

DIVING
BRITISH
VIRGIN ISLANDS

By Jim And Odile Scheiner

AQUA QUEST PUBLICATIONS, INC. ▪ NEW YORK

PUBLISHER'S NOTE

The Aqua Quest *Diving* series offers extensive information on dive sites as well as topside activities.

At the time of publication, the information contained in this book was determined to be as accurate and up-to-date as possible. The reader should bear in mind, however, that dive site terrain and landmarks change due to weather or construction. In addition, new dive shops, restaurants, hotels and stores can open and existing ones close. Telephone numbers are subject to change as are government regulations.

The publisher welcomes the reader's comments and assistance to help ensure the accuracy of future editions of this book.

Good diving and enjoy your stay!

Library of Congress Cataloging-in-Publication Data

Scheiner, James B.
    Diving British Virgin Islands / by Jim and Odile Scheiner.
        p.   cm.   — (Aqua Quest diving series)
    Includes index.
    ISBN 0-9623389-6-6 : $18.95 (alk. paper)
    1. Scuba diving—British Virgin Islands—Guidebooks. 2.
British Virgin Islands—Guidebooks. I. Scheiner, Odile.
II. Title. III. Series
GV840.S782B756 1996
797.2'3—dc20
                                    96-8728
                                    CIP

Cover: The brilliance of the technicolor sponges at Painted Walls is brought out by the photographer's strobe.

Title page: A charter yacht anchors off Sandy Spit, one of the many isolated beaches awaiting exploration.

Printed in Hong Kong
10 9 8 7 6 5 4 3 2 1

Design by Richard Liu.

ACKNOWLEDGEMENTS

We would like to thank the BVI dive operators who have graciously tolerated our long photo dives for so many years; especially Baskin in the Sun, Blue Water Divers, *Cuan Law*, Dive BVI and Underwater Safaris. Many thanks to the many individual dive guides we have discussed the dive sites with; especially Sue Thompson, Randy Keil, Pete Foster, Chuck Gathers and Kim Clayton.

DEDICATION

To the memories of
Martin Scheiner and Kathleen Long

Contents

[handwritten margin note: Great Harbor center of Bay 20 yds from shore 8'–18'–40']

(handwritten notes)

Scrub Island
S. side reef
<60'

Little Camaroe
NE tip
30' reef dives
coral
overhangs
nground seas

Van Ryais
Rock
98 collison ft.
lobsters, turtles
fish, coral, fans

Joe's cave

Ginger Island
Mushroom coral
15-20' high
70-90'
stingrays, jewfish

FOREWORD

Columbus passed through in 1493, and other than a few nefarious pirates and ill-fated plantations, the British Virgin Islands remained relatively untouched for the next 500 years.

But now, at the dawn of the 21st century, the BVI has been "rediscovered" by discerning divers and yachtsmen. Unique in all the Caribbean, with over 50 islands and islets, the BVI offers extraordinary vacation opportunities. Pristine and undeveloped, there's not a single traffic light or fast food franchise. With professional services widely available, this British Dependent Territory offers a back-to-nature experience with all the modern comforts. Uninhabited islands, sunken wrecks, secluded coves, treasure caves, exquisite beaches, and thickly wooded slopes await the adventurous and laid-back alike.

BVI diving is renowned for its variety and bountifulness. From the sunken island of Anegada, with over 300 known wrecks, to the Dogs off Virgin Gorda; from the popular dive at The Indians to the remote sites off Jost Van Dyke, there is always a new and exciting site to explore. The most famous dive is the wreck of the 310-foot (94 m) RMS *Rhone* which sank off Salt Island in 1867. This iron-hulled steam and sail ship was a technological masterpiece in its day. Today, it fascinates divers with its sense of history and abundant fish life. Throughout the BVI healthy reefs and thriving fish populations abound and will continue to do so because of the conservation efforts of the government, dive operators and National Parks Trust, including a territory-wide dive-site mooring system.

This guidebook is the most extensive one available for divers and snorkelers, covering over 50 sites, with maps pinpointing these areas. While we suggest that most of these dives be done with a local diving professional, we have attempted to provide enough information to assist the experienced diver/boat handler in planning their own dives. For each site you will find information about required skill level, location of dive site mooring, nearest anchorage, suitability for snorkeling and currents, in addition to a comprehensive site description.

Since there is so much more to the BVI than just the underwater realm, we have included extensive coverage of the topside world. An island-by-island description of both natural attractions, and restaurants and hotels, along with a brief historical overlook, will assist in planning your vacation and help maximize your enjoyment when here.

Tortola has been our home for over 15 years. We have logged thousands of dives throughout the archipelago and spent time on every island. We are excited about this book because it allows us, finally, to share our insider's knowledge with more than just a select few visiting divers and yachtsmen.

We hope you enjoy this book as much as we did "researching" it. When you visit the BVI, make sure you come by our Photo Center and say hello.

Jim & Odile Scheiner
Road Town, Tortola
April 1997

CHAPTER I BRITISH VIRGIN ISLANDS

THE PAST

Centuries before the voyages of Columbus, at least three other groups explored these islands. The nomadic stone age Chiboney Indians are the first recorded visitors. They were followed, almost two thousand years ago, by the Arawaks who worked their way up from South America in dugout canoes. These peaceful Indians established farming communities and lived in quiet harmony on the undefiled island paradises they found. A hundred or so years before Columbus, the fierce Carib Indians swept through, attacking Arawak settlements, enslaving or eating those who didn't flee. Today the Arawaks are no more. Those who survived the Caribs eventually died as slaves to the conquering Spanish, who themselves were subject to raids by the Caribs—the Caribbean's first pirates. Only a small remnant of Carib Indians still clings to their ancestral identity high in the hills of Dominica.

On his second epic voyage in 1493, Columbus "discovered" the Virgin Islands, landing at Salt River Bay in St. Croix to take on water. Sailing through these waters he was so inspired by the sheer number of little islands and cays clustered about the larger ones that he named them *Las Once Mil Virgines* (The 11,000 Virgins) after the legend of St. Ursula and her 11,000 virgin martyrs who chose death rather than be defiled by marauding Huns in 4th-century Europe.

Financed by the vast gold treasure they took out of South America, the Spanish quickly began to rule the Caribbean, although they ignored the Virgin Islands in favor of the more fertile larger islands and the South American mainland. The other European nations, not willing to challenge Spain directly, commissioned civilian ships as privateers, authorizing them to ransack Spanish ships and settlements. In practice there wasn't much difference between the official privateers and outlaw pirates, especially to the ships they plundered. The Virgin Islands, spurned by early settlers for their dearth of flat arable land, were a haven for these pirates due to the multitude of hidden bays and lookout hills, and proximity to the trade routes of heavily laden merchant ships. The names of these pirates still fire the imagination today: Henry Morgan, Blackbeard, Sir John Hawkins—even Sir Francis Drake was a government-sponsored privateer. Their presence lives on in local place names: Norman Island, Jost van Dyke, the several Thatch Islands (named for Blackbeard, a.k.a. Teach or Thatch), Dead Chest Island and of course the Sir Francis Drake Channel.

As the source of their stolen gold petered out, Spanish dominance over the region weakened, and England, France, Denmark and Holland began to expand their colonial footholds in the New World. Many of the islands, including the Virgins, passed from one flag to another. The Dutch are credited with the first permanent settlement, at Soper's Hole in 1648. In 1672 the English, realizing the increasing strategic value of the Virgin Islands, ousted the Dutch and took possession of Tortola and Virgin Gorda. Denmark got St. Thomas, and later St. John and St. Croix, until the United States purchased all three US Virgin Islands in 1917.

In the late 1600's the economy of the Virgin Islands began to shift from piracy and plunder to agriculture. Though the first farmers on Tortola remained confirmed part time pirates, sugarcane and cotton plantations were soon

Part of the fun of visiting the BVI is exploring the secluded anchorages and beautiful beaches such as Sandy Spit.

carved out of the steep hillsides. Fueled by the raw manpower of African slaves, the BVI entered a period of prosperity.

During this plantation era two native sons rose to prominence. Dr. John Coakley Lettsom was born on Jost Van Dyke in 1744. Though he freed his slaves and founded the London Medical Society, he is best remembered for his poetry:

> I, John Lettsom
> Blisters, Bleeds and Sweats 'em,
> If, after that, they please to die,
> I, John Lettsom

William Thornton, also born in the BVI, went on to design the US Capitol Building in Washington, DC.

Eventually the plantation system began to disintegrate due to the introduction of the sugar beet in Europe. Droughts, hurricanes, European and American wars, as well as the inevitable decline of the institution of slavery also contributed. Emancipation came to Tortola's slaves in 1834. (Today the annual August Festival celebrates this day of liberation.) Many continued to work on the same plantations for the same owners, but now as free men. However, conditions did not improve, and in 1853 there was a major insurrection of former slaves. They burned the great houses and fields, and destroyed the sugar works. In the aftermath, virtually all the whites fled the islands and the land was abandoned to the forefathers of today's BV Islanders. The ruins of estate sugar mills and distilleries can still be seen today.

For the next 100 years the BVI slept on undisturbed, going "back to bush." It is this long period of isolation and possession of the land that has given today's BV Islander so much quiet pride and dignity, as well as a great sense of independence and self-reliance. The dawn of the 20th century brought few changes. English colonial government returned. And as there was no local industry and not much agriculture, most men went to St. Thomas and Puerto Rico to look for work. In 1967 a new constitution provided for a locally elected ministerial system of government headed by a chief minister, along with a governor appointed by England. The island group remains a Dependent Territory, under British control.

The construction of Laurance Rockefeller's luxury resort at Little Dix Bay, Virgin Gorda in the early 1960's marks the beginning of the modern tourist economy. The Moorings chartered their first "bareboat" in 1969 and tourist development has been slow but steady ever since.

THE PRESENT

The British Virgin Islands lie like crown jewels atop the emerald chain of diminutive Caribbean islands that stretches northward from South America, separating the Atlantic Ocean from the Caribbean Sea. These islands are the remains of ancient submerged volcanoes that were thrust above the surface of the ocean by the primal forces of plate tectonics during the turbulent adolescence of our planet.

Now the British Virgin Islands bask peacefully in the tropical sun just 60 miles (97 km) east of Puerto Rico, and far removed from the hustle and bustle of the modern world. Geologically the BVI are part of the same archipelago that includes the adjacent US Virgin Islands. While there are many bonds of family and commerce that tie the US Virgins and British Virgin Islands together, they are a world apart in terms of ambiance and vacation experience. Until recently the BVI was overshadowed by the more developed and heavily promoted USVI. But these pristine islands have now come into their own, and offer world class facilities and services against a backdrop of unspoiled natural beauty.

There are over 36 islands, and numerous rocks and cays in the BVI, comprising a total land mass of 59 square miles (152 sq km). The BVI boasts a tremendous variety of topography including gently rolling hills, cloud-kissed mountain peaks, palm tree-lined beaches, cactus-studded bluffs, offshore pinnacles, secluded bays and sheer cliffs. Sixteen of the larger islands are inhabited. The principal ones are Tortola, Virgin Gorda, Jost Van Dyke and Anegada. Peter, Cooper and Salt Islands, as well as Guana, Great Camanoe, Necker and Mosquito, host small populations. The 1991 census counted over 16,000 people in the territory.

The mainstay of the economy is tourism. But it's not the hustling tourism of hi-rises and casinos. There are no fast food franchises or

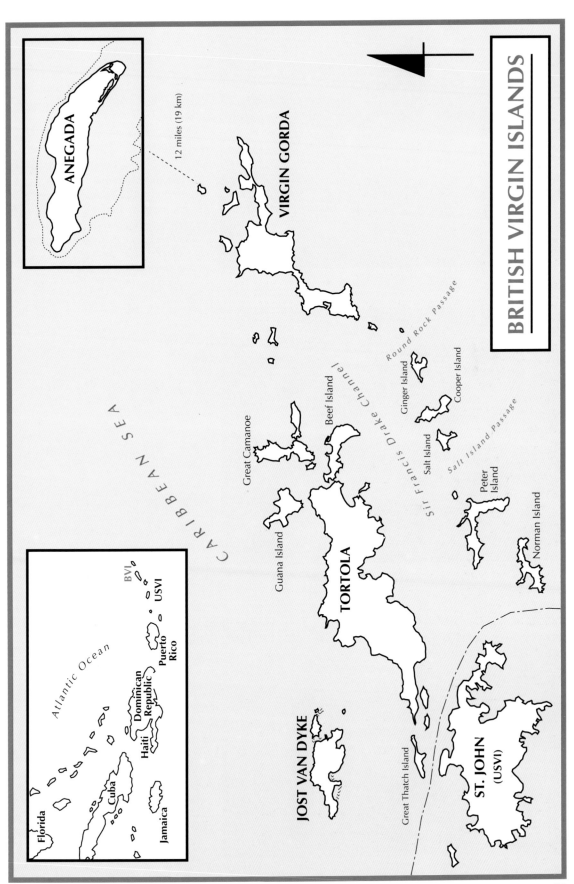

ANEGADA

12 miles (19 km)

VIRGIN GORDA

Round Rock Passage

Ginger Island

Cooper Island

Beef Island

Salt Island

Sir Francis Drake Channel

Salt Island Passage

Great Camanoe

Peter Island

CARIBBEAN SEA

Norman Island

Guana Island

TORTOLA

JOST VAN DYKE

Great Thatch Island

ST. JOHN
(USVI)

Atlantic Ocean

BVI

USVI

Puerto Rico

Dominican Republic

Haiti

Cuba

Florida

Jamaica

BRITISH VIRGIN ISLANDS

Uninhabited Norman Island was once a notorious pirate hideout. Lookouts stationed on Spy Glass Hill could watch for ships in all directions. Pirate booty has been recovered from the caves on Treasure Point.

Though the flower lasts only a day, hibiscus is a favorite plant among BVI gardeners. Bougainvillea, frangipani and oleander also add splashes of color to green hillsides.

Powered by the constant tradewinds caressing the islands, windsurfing is very popular. Several schools offer instruction and rentals. Annual regattas and inter-island commuting provide the challenge.

hotel chains, not even a traffic light. Years before the word "eco-tourism" was coined, let alone turned into advertising hype, the British Virgin Islands was in the vanguard. Yacht chartering, with its minimal environmental impact and inherent appreciation of a pristine environment, has long been the primary industry of these islands.

Scuba diving is now catching up. For many years the beautiful varied reefs and exceptional wrecks were known only to a few intrepid divers. But word of mouth has slowly made the BVI one of today's hottest diving destinations.

Taxes and fees generated by offshore Trust Companies (International Business Companies or IBC's) contribute greatly to government coffers. These companies, often consisting of little more than a company seal in a rack of hundreds of other seals in a lawyer's or accountant's office, are increasing rapidly.

The overall pace of development is quickening. Visitors returning after an absence of just a couple of years are often astonished at the amount of construction and new businesses. All of this contributes to one of the most prosperous economies in the region with almost 100 percent employment. This prosperity has led to increased local ownership of businesses.

Local businessmen and foreign investors enjoy the political stability of the BVI's British Dependent Territory status. Representatives to the Legislative Council are elected from each of nine separate districts. They then form a ministerial government overseen by a governor who is sent from England. A very imposing administrative building was recently erected on the waterfront in Road Town.

USEFUL INFORMATION

Climate. The BVI is blessed with an almost perfect climate. The warmth of the tropical sun is tempered by the constant trade winds. The temperature varies from 75°F to 85°F (24°C-29°C) in the winter and 80°F to 90°F (27°C-32°C) in the summer. With a drop of 10°F in the evening, even summer nights are very comfortable. As you ascend up the hills, the temperature drops dramatically, so if you're staying in a house on the hillside, make sure you bring some warm clothes for the evenings, especially in winter.

Getting There. Most visitors from North America fly into San Juan, Puerto Rico and then take a 30-minute shuttle flight to the BVI. The American Airlines to American Eagle shuttle connection is very good; bags and passengers generally make it on their scheduled flights. An alternate route is to fly into St. Thomas and then take a shuttle flight or, more enjoyably, take one of the many ferry boats that travel between St. Thomas and Tortola. Cruising up the Sir Francis Drake Channel, wind in your hair, sun on your face, watching the islands and yachts pass by is a perfect introduction to the BVI.

Entry and Exit Requirements. A passport is always recommended for international travel, but American and Canadian citizens can enter with other legitimate proof of citizenship. Six months is the maximum stay allowed (but one month is usually the maximum granted on arrival). All visitors must be prepared to show return or ongoing tickets, prearranged accommodations and evidence of adequate means of support. A departure tax of $10.00 per person leaving by air and $5.00 per person leaving by sea is charged.

Currency, Taxes and Fees. The coin of the realm is the US dollar, so there aren't any exchange rate complications. Major credit cards are accepted in many, but not all establishments, so it's worth inquiring before you run up a big bill at a restaurant.

While there is no sales tax, there is a 10-cent government duty on every check and traveler's check. A 7 percent hotel accommodation tax and a 10 percent service fee are charged at hotels. Import duty (from 5 to 22 percent) is often charged on luxury items brought into the territory, though temporary visitors are normally exempt. The yacht charter companies collect a cruising permit fee for all charters.

The National Parks Trust (NPT) charges for their Marine Conservation (Moorings) Permit; the rates vary according to the type of boat. This permit is necessary if you want to use the dive site moorings. The NPT also charges a dollar a day for each diver on the commercial dive boats—the dive shops collect this from visiting divers. These National Parks tariffs bypass the government General Fund and go directly to the National Parks Trust to help pay for mooring maintenance, educational programs and reef protection enforcement.

Spinnakers fly in the annual BVI Spring Regatta. Sailors come from all over the region to compete and party.

Small racing catamarans offer big boat sailors the chance to go fast and compete against one another in the annual CAT BVI regatta.

Electricity. Electricity is 110 volts, 60 cycles just like it is in the United States. No transformers or plug adapters are required. The power is reasonably stable and dependable enough for charging batteries.

Telephone. The BVI has good, though rather expensive, phone service. International direct dialing service is available. Cable & Wireless, the local phone company, permits charging calls to major credit cards as well as offering "USA Direct" via AT&T. Local calls are made by dialing the five-digit number. To call the BVI from the States dial 1-809-49 followed by the five-digit local number. Fax machines are proliferating and several dive companies offer 800 numbers that ring directly in their on-island reservation offices.

To call 800 numbers from the BVI, don't dial the "1" in front of the 800. There is a 45-cent per minute charge for these "toll free" numbers, and not all 800 numbers are accessible.

In addition, CCT Boat Phone offers cellular phone service throughout the BVI. In fact, they have installed phones on many charter boats

Small, adorable and rarely seen, tiny tree frogs celebrate the rain with a nighttime serenade.

which are activated with a simple call to their operator and a credit card number. While it's obscenely expensive, many folks get great pleasure by calling the office from their yacht to say, "You'll never guess where I'm calling from."

Time. The BVI is on Atlantic Standard Time, which is one hour ahead of Eastern Standard. Since the territory doesn't observe Daylight Saving, in the summer it's effectively the same time as Eastern Daylight.

Driving and Transportation. If using American left-side-drive cars and driving on the left side of the road (as in Europe) wasn't intimidating enough, wait 'til you see how they drive here. There are no traffic lights in the BVI and the roads are pretty much a free-for-all, where size is more important than right-of-way.

Island tours of Tortola or Virgin Gorda are quite enjoyable. Renting a car or jeep is a great way to see the island at your own pace; but please drive carefully on the steep hills and always drive defensively. And remember to keep left. Temporary licenses are required and available at the Traffic Licensing Office and car rental agencies. For the faint of heart, taxis and tour buses are readily available.

Inter-island ferries link Tortola, Virgin Gorda

AUGUST FESTIVAL

Celebrating the emancipation from slavery in 1834, this half-month-long festival starts with the construction of Festival Village in Road Town in late July. It includes nightly entertainment by local musicians playing steelband, fungi and calypso music. Other festival highlights include the Prince and Princess Show, the Calypso Show and the Miss BVI Show. Local foods (johnny cake, meat patties, conch fritters, bull foot stew and mutton) and local drinks (maubi, bacardi) can be purchased at the Festival Village. While the Festival Village is open during the day it doesn't really get moving until late at night. As Festival Monday (the first Monday in August) approaches the pace and exuberance build, culminating in the Grand Parade on Monday. The parade, complete with floats, lots of live music, dancing troupes and "mocho jumbies" on stilts, winds slowly through Road Town and finishes at the Village. It's a fun, colorful day and the whole island comes to a stop to enjoy it.

and Jost Van Dyke, as well as the USVI and BVI. Ferry service is also available to Peter and Cooper Islands. "Day Sail" boats can take you virtually anywhere in the archipelago. Fly BVI, a private air charter company, can fly you anywhere or just take you around for a scenic aerial tour.

Island Sensibilities. BV Islanders tend to be a little shy and retiring. It is usually necessary for you to break the ice first with a casual greeting and some sort of conversational follow up. Once a person has gotten to know you, you'll find their sense of humor and personal warmth to be very fulfilling. Long and lasting friendships are often forged between repeat visitors and the islanders they've met over the years. Most Tortolians don't appreciate being photographed without being asked first—it's just common courtesy.

The BVI is a fairly informal place; jackets are required in only a few of the toniest dinner establishments. Casual but clean will get you in most anywhere. However, bare feet, short shorts, bare midriffs, skimpy attire, shirtless men and bathing suits in general are not appreciated in town or along the roads. It is requested that you wear your beach attire on the beaches only. Nudity is illegal.

Language. The official language is English, however, among themselves the islanders speak an almost indecipherable calypso dialect. It's musical to the ears, but at best you'll only understand a few words. When talking to visitors most islanders switch to English, and even then you might have some trouble understanding.

Shopping. While not a duty-free shopping mecca like its neighbor St. Thomas, the BVI does offer its share of shopping experiences. Very few products are actually made in the Territory, but many of the stores sell high quality West Indian-style items. In Road Town most of the shops are clustered along charming Main Street with its traditional gingerbread houses. Pussers, Sunny Caribee and Serendipity are among the most popular. Virgin Gorda offers shopping in Spanish Town and at its many resorts.

Where to Stay. There are so many options that an entire book could be written on where to stay. Each island has its own personality: unspoiled Jost Van Dyke, quiet but sophisticated Virgin Gorda, away-from-it-all Anegada and just-want-to-have-fun Tortola. The style and range of accommodations runs from large all-inclusive luxury resorts and

August Festival ostensibly commemorates the end of slavery in 1834, but today it is more of a celebration of being a BV Islander. Native sons come home from all over the world to party with friends and family. The parade on August Monday is the highlight of the festivities, with many revelers in exquisite costumes.

quaint inns, to funky-but-elegant seaside hotels and rental villas. There are no hi-rises or condos, just pleasant cottages and holiday homes. Afloat, your options include live-aboard dive boats, chartered luxury yachts or bareboats. Many visitors split their time between land and sea: spending part of their vacation on a boat and staying ashore for a few days on each end of their charter. Contact the BVI Tourist Board listed in the Appendix for literature, or call one of the dive shops directly and they'll help you find the perfect place for your needs and budget.

What to Do. While the BVI is a very upscale destination, most activities revolve around the natural beauty of the islands and the sea. There are no casinos, golf courses, few cruise ships and limited night life. With a fleet of almost a thousand boats, the BVI is the charter boat capital of the world. Sailing, diving, snorkeling and island exploration are the main activities. If your vacation isn't pre-planned with a yacht charter or dive package, part of the fun will be discovering all the activities available: from day sailing and windsurfing, to hiking, tennis and horseback riding, and of course, island hopping and sun bathing.

Come evening, most people are so tired from a day spent out in the sun and under the sea, that a big night out is a fine meal and a quiet walk under the stars. For those who aren't quite ready for bed, there is usually a band playing somewhere or perhaps a darts game. If you come to the BVI looking for wild night life or all inclusive resort-style vacations, you'll be disappointed.

CHAPTER II DIVING

One of the great pleasures of diving in the BVI is the variety of dive sites. There are lush coral gardens, gently sloping reefs, sheer mini-walls, exciting sea mounts, fantastic wrecks, coral-encrusted boulder fields, tunnels, ledges—no two sites are alike. There are well over 70 established dive sites and many more when you take into account the "secret" sites of individual dive guides and boat captains.

There are also many different styles of BVI diving: resort-based commercial dive boat, crewed liveaboard, rendezvous diving, or doing it on your own from a bareboat. No matter what you choose, the support facilities and personnel are all professional and first class.

As most of the dive sites are on the smaller uninhabited islands and pinnacles spread out along the Sir Francis Drake Channel, a boat is required to reach them. Travel to and from the sites is always a treat as you voyage on a sea dotted with beautiful yachts, great clipper ships and inter-island ferries.

The most popular sites are buoyed with National Parks Trust moorings and are relatively easy to find once you're in the immediate vicinity. But even with the dive site moorings and help from this book, enlisting local knowledge goes a long way to ensuring a rewarding and safe diving experience. We sincerely recommend that you dive with a local professional; the experience will be easier, safer and more enjoyable.

Types Of Diving

Topography. The turbulent geological history of these islands is revealed in many of the BVI's unique dive sites. Some are slashed by high-walled narrow rock canyons and tunnels, or littered with giant car- and condo-sized boulders. Still others are pockmarked with small caves and alcoves, and encrusted with brilliantly colored sponges.

The majority of dive sites lie just offshore on gently sloping reefs. The spur-and-groove pattern of reef formation is typical of sites such as Dead Chest West and Alice in Wonderland. This topography is one of high coral ridges running perpendicular to shore, interspersed with sand channels. Another variation are coral steps or terraces descending seaward. Depths range from 20 feet (6 m) near shore to 60 to 80 feet (18-24 m) further seaward.

Some of the more spectacular dives are the offshore sea mounts with dramatic ledges and undercuts to explore. Blonde Rock, Santa Monica Rock and Carrot Shoal all boast thick clouds of fishes and the possibility of encounters with larger pelagic fish, such as amberjacks, kingfish and cobia.

While the BVI doesn't boast sheer drop-offs descending into fathomless blue, there still are many inviting mini-walls. Starting in 25 to 35 feet (8-9 m) of water they usually bottom out at 65 to 100 feet (20-30 m). The coral walls of Spy Glass and Truck Reef are covered with purple tube sponges, black coral and schools of delicate tropical fishes.

Skill Levels. Complementing the geographic variety of the dive sites is a corresponding variety in difficulty. There are many sites that are perfect for first time resort course divers.

However, there are some sites that can be rather challenging due to location, open water conditions, currents or navigational complexity. These are best left to more

Trumpetfish are active predators and often use the structures of the reef as camouflage when they stalk smaller fishes.

Queen angels are the shyest of the angelfishes. Their exquisite colors and regal crown endear them to photographers.

experienced divers or done with a professional dive guide, or on certain days, forsaken for calmer sites. The water conditions can change from day to day or even hour to hour.

Due to their remoteness from land, some sites (Santa Monica Rock, the Invisibles, Watson Rock, the *Chikuzen*) are always considered advanced. Out there it is necessary to navigate back to the boat (preferably underwater) or risk being swept out to sea. There is no close shore to swim to when things get out of control and not many boats passing by to flag down for assistance. These sites are obviously best done with a guide.

Overall, most sites are easily dived by a moderately experienced diver in reasonable physical condition, especially when accompanied by a dive guide. We have tried to evaluate each site according to required skill level. But due to the variables of water conditions and each diver's individual strength and experience, this is an approximation at best.

Snorkeling (S). There is such an abundance of spectacular and bountiful shallow reefs that for many, mask and fins suffice as a hassle-free way to enjoy the marine world. Unlike diving, there are many snorkel sites easily accessible from shore. Those on the northern coasts of the islands can be exposed to dangerously large sea swells and undertows during the winter months.

As with the dive sites, the majority and the best snorkeling locations are reachable only by boat. "Day Sail" boats out of Tortola and Virgin Gorda can take you to some of the more popular sites—the Caves, the Indians and the Baths—as well as their own secret spots. Commercial dive boats usually welcome snorkelers onboard, depending on the suitability of the day's destination.

We have indicated with an **(S)** the dive sites which are suitable for snorkeling. In addition, there are many quiet bays and lee sides of points that offer very rewarding snorkeling. Just floating over an ordinary eel-grass bed can reveal an entirely new marine habitat with rays patrolling, turtles feeding, conch marching and the juveniles of many of the reef fishes hiding in the shadows. Though less inviting, mangroves are another ecosystem worthy of snorkel exploration.

Shore Diving. Unfortunately, there are few dive sites in the BVI that are accessible from a shore you're likely to be on. The northern shore of Brewer's Bay in Tortola and Cistern Point on Cooper Island are exceptions. With all the different kinds of boat diving available, the loss of the independence of shore diving is a small price to pay. There are boats to meet most every budget. Furthermore, there are many fine snorkeling reefs around Tortola and Virgin Gorda accessible from shore.

Wreck Diving. Every certified diver has heard of the wreck of the RMS *Rhone* and it certainly is worthy of its fame; however, there are many other excellent wreck dives in the BVI. The *Chikuzen* lies north of Tortola, out in the Atlantic Ocean, and is an excellent big fish wreck; the *Marie L*, near Cooper Island, promises a possible jewfish encounter; and the *Fearless*, off Peter Island, is surrounded by a reef adorned by black coral. Recent arrivals include a 70-foot (21 m) tugboat and a nondescript hull placed adjacent to the *Marie L* and the Atlantic Air BVI airplane off Great

Dog. The Willie T, formerly a very popular floating bar and restaurant off Norman Island, is now sitting on the ocean floor near the Fearless. Anegada's treacherous Horse Shoe Reef has ripped the bottoms from hundreds of vessels. While most have long since succumbed to the destructive forces of the sea, there are several good and less dived wrecks to be found there.

Boat Diving. All the best sites are accessible by boat and many are reachable solely by boat. Dive operators generally frequent sites within a half-hour of their base, though longer runs to more exotic sites such as the *Chikuzen* are common. Most sites are located in protected water, but the boat ride to get there can occasionally be rough, so divers prone to seasickness should take precautions.

The local commercial dive boats are very well designed with large dive platforms, integral tank racks, ascent/descent lines, and surface current tag lines. Some even offer

Snorkeling is a favorite pastime for sailors and landlubbers alike. The fishes at the Caves and at many other sites are often approachable.

horizontal hang bars at 15 feet (5 m) for a safety stop.

Boat Diving On Your Own. With the advent of the NPT dive site moorings, more and more divers are heading out on chartered bareboats with a rack full of tanks to do their own thing. Great! However, diving from a boat without professional supervision in unfamiliar waters is more complicated than many newcomers realize. Sailboats are not especially well suited for use as a diving platform and if you do get in trouble, there is nobody there (at least initially) to bail you out. In addition to prudent common sense and standard safe diving practices, here are a few hints for safer diving.

- **Select an appropriate dive site.** Bear in mind the ocean conditions, your experience level and your physical condition. If the site of your dreams is too advanced for you, consider rendezvousing with one of the dive operators—they'll look after you.
- **Plan ahead.** Have some sort of dive plan and a backup plan. It's best to leave someone on board who can operate your boat, or at least the dinghy, and who knows radio procedures. That way they can come get you if necessary or call for help if things really get out of hand. And please, don't forget to lower the ladder or some other means to get back on board. Sometimes it's easier to climb back into the dinghy first. With the amount of boat traffic in these water, it is imperative that you fly a big obvious dive flag.
- **Check for current.** Currents are generally stronger on the surface and in mid-water than they are on the bottom. Avoid drifting away. Use a tag or current line to hold on to while you are on the surface. You can also use this line to pull yourself back to the boat if you surface behind the boat. A weighted ascent/descent line greatly minimizes the complications of current. How it hangs in the water column will also help indicate presence and strength of currents. Please keep the line short enough so that it won't hit and damage the sea floor. Once on the bottom start your dive up current and stay low to the bottom to minimize your exposure to the flowing water. If the current is too strong, don't dive.

- **Navigation.** It is always best to return to your boat underwater and avoid problems with surface conditions, boat traffic and fatigue. If you're not familiar with the site or your navigation skills are mediocre, keep it simple and don't stray far from your boat. There is no need to try to see an entire reef on one dive. It's easiest to navigate back to the mooring pin; it won't move and you can't swim under it without seeing it, like you can a boat. It is always a good idea to inspect the mooring hardware for wear and chafe anyway. The simplest way to navigate back to the mooring is to look back at it and other landmarks as you swim away, so you know what to look for as you return. Make a few mental notes of any special topographical features.
- **Try to return to the boat underwater.** Even if you have to surface to take bearings, make sure you have enough air to do the final swim underwater— it's safer and much easier. Anytime you surface away from the boat, stop, look and listen before you make the final ascent. While you can hear power boats, sailboats make no noise and their lead-filled keels reach down six feet (2 m). A 3- to 10-minute safety stop at 15 feet (5 m) is always a good idea. A diver safety "sausage" is easy to carry rolled up in a BC pocket, and when inflated sticks up 6 feet (2 m) out of the water, making it much easier to find you if you're drifting on the surface.
- **Take it slow and easy.** Don't be afraid to ask for advice or information from a local diving professional. They're only too happy to help. They want all BVI diving experiences to be fun and safe.

Night Diving. By the far the most popular night dive is the wreck of the *Rhone*. Venturing inside the fairly intact bow section at 70 feet

(21 m) is an exciting experience. The colors seem to explode as your dive light illuminates the fully-open orange cup coral against a background of blood-red encrusting sponge. Sleeping fishes are easily approached. Fishes and creatures that hide during the day come out to feed. Lobsters venture out into the open, moray eels are seen sniffing out prey, and the eyes of countless nocturnal shrimps glow red in the beam of your light. If you're lucky, you might spot an octopus on the prowl, its probing tentacles adroitly exploring every nook and cranny for a midnight snack.

If you're diving with a commercial dive operator or from a dedicated liveaboard, they'll probably have all the necessary equipment. However, if you're doing it on your own, here are a couple of suggestions: Keep it simple, dive a site you've been on in daylight, and chose a location with no current and moderate depths. The Indians, Diamond Reef (off Marina Cay) and Cistern Point at Cooper Island are all diver-friendly night dives.

Dusk is one of our favorite times to dive. Slip into the water just before sunset and witness the heightened activity on the reef as predators take advantage of the failing light and slightly confused fishes. Then watch as the daytime creatures disperse and the nocturnal animals claim the reef.

CONDITIONS

Season. The BVI is diveable all year round. The seas are generally calm and even when they're not, it is always possible to find a protected calm-water dive site. During the winter months the water is cooler and the Christmas Winds and north swell (caused by winter storms in the North Atlantic) can make crossing the Sir Francis Drake Channel a little rougher and limit the selection of dive sites slightly, but the diver is often rewarded with generally better visibility. There are many days when it's mill-pond calm in the middle of winter.

In summer the water is calmer, opening more sites, including the north side, to exploration. Visibility can drop, as do the prices and crowds. Spring and fall are also great times to visit; the dive boats and anchorages are almost deserted, and the diving is outstanding. Late August, September and October are the height of hurricane season.

Historically the BVI has been bypassed by most hurricanes and with today's accurate tracking and prediction there is no reason not to visit during this time. Many restaurants and smaller guest houses close during September.

Currents and Winds. Due to minimal tides there is little or no tidal current at most inshore dive sites. However, the BVI is bathed by the larger Equatorial Current coming from the southeast. This current usually brings in clear water. Dive sites located in passes between islands or on projections of land can experience significant current, especially if the tidal flow and offshore current are flowing in the same direction. On occasion, the current can be so strong that moving to another, more sheltered site is the prudent choice. It is almost impossible to predict the currents, and with variable combinations of the two, the overall flow can change direction, increase or die at any moment. With a little bit of common sense and some current diving experience, the currents do not pose a significant problem.

Steady tradewinds are one of the reasons that the BVI has become such a popular sailing destination. Their gentle cooling effect is much appreciated and the consistency of their direction (out of the southeast) allows for predicable dive site selection. Normally their influence is minimal, however, sometimes during the winter months the Christmas Winds pick up. Blowing steadily at 15-20 knots, with stronger gusts, these winds can kick up surface chop on the usually tranquil Sir Francis Drake Channel and make some of the more exposed dive sites less than inviting. But you'll never be completely blown out, as there is always a lee shore to dive.

Depth. The diving in the BVI is generally fairly shallow, with 80 feet (24 m) considered a deeper dive. In many locations the most interesting topography is right along the shoreline in 40 feet (12 m) or less. These shallow areas also offer the brightest colors and longest dives.

Visibility. Visibility averages in the 60- to 100-foot range (18-30 m). Generally it's a little clearer in winter and slightly more obscured by plankton in summer. The plankton that limits visibility feeds the rich invertebrate life that makes the reefs in the BVI so bountiful.

Water Temperature. The water temperature varies from a low of 77-79°F (25-26°C) in

How To Use The Mooring System

1. Approach slowly from downwind. Choose an appropriately colored mooring ball (see regulations).
2. Have someone in the bow direct the helmsman and have a boat hook ready.
3. Try to be dead in the water when picking up the mooring pennant.
4. It is vital to loop a 10- to 20-foot (3-6 m) line through the eye of the mooring pennant and then attach each end of that line to your bow cleats. The increased scope will decrease the upward pull on the mooring pin cemented in the bottom, as well as dramatically reduce chafe on the pickup pennant.
5. It is always a good idea to inspect the mooring hardware for wear or damage before you swim off and leave your boat. It is also a wise precaution to leave someone on board in case a problem does occur with the mooring.
6. When leaving the mooring, simply pull your added line through the pennant and then let the wind blow you back away from the mooring before putting your engine in gear. Most damage to the moorings is done by running them over on departure.

winter to a high of 82-84°F (28-29°C) in summer. In summer or early fall, a shorty dive skin or just a t-shirt should do fine. If you're doing a lot of repetitive diving or get cold easily, we recommend that you wear a full suit of some kind. A skin usually isn't enough in winter. An eighth-inch (3 mm) wetsuit or one of the new three-ply laminate suits with a "chicken vest" underneath should suffice.

Preserving Paradise

Moorings. A system of moorings has been installed by the National Parks Trust in virtually all of the most popular dive sites to prevent damage to the reef from anchors. The program, started by the BVI Dive Operators Association, plans to eventually have over 250 moorings in place. The moorings are based on the "Halas Method" of drilling holes in the sea floor and cementing a large stainless steel pin in place. Because a chafe-protected floating line leads directly from the pin to a mooring ball on the surface, there is absolutely no damage to the surrounding reef.

In addition to the National Parks Trust moorings, private companies, such as Moor Seacure Ltd., have placed moorings at many of the popular overnight anchorages. These, for a fee, provide yachtsmen peace of mind through the night, as well as preservation of the sea grass ecosystem.

Regulations regarding National Parks Trust moorings:

- A nominal user fee must be paid. The revenue goes directly to the National Parks Trust to be used for mooring installation and maintenance, and not into the Government's General Fund.
- Vessel must have NPT permit.
- Maximum allowed length of vessel is 50 feet (15 m).
- Yellow mooring floats are for commercial dive boats only.
- Orange/red mooring floats are for general day use.
- White mooring floats are "for recreational or commercial vessels while actively diving" only. There is a

90-minute limit. A dive flag must be flown. Do not use these moorings for snorkeling or lunch stops. Once the dive is over, please vacate the mooring immediately as other vessels may be determining site availability from a considerable distance.

■ Blue mooring floats are for dinghies.
■ No overnight use of any NPT mooring.
■ All moorings are on a first come, first served basis.
■ No anchoring in National Marine Park areas.

Conservation Regulations. The National Parks Trust and the Department of Conservation and Fisheries have established a set of laws that serve to protect the marine environment and its inhabitants.

It is illegal to remove any flora or fauna from the ocean floor. Collection of marine products with scuba is strictly forbidden. This includes lobsters, conch, corals and fishes.

Fishing with hook and line is permitted only with a visitor's Temporary Fishing Permit, and not in protected areas. The permit costs approximately $20 and is available from the Department of Conservation and Fisheries in Road Town.

Being A Kinder, Gentler Diver. There is a lot that each of us can do to minimize our own individual wear and tear on the fragile reef and its inhabitants. It is exceedingly easy to damage coral. The thin layer of living tissue over the stony coral skeleton is very susceptible to injury from abrasion and the fragile branching corals are easily broken. Once abraded or broken, colonizing algae or infection can attack the coral and, if it is in a weakened condition, kill it. The guiding principle should be that of making little or no physical contact with the reef—look but don't touch.

Proper buoyancy control is a great start. Divers wearing too much lead and those simply out of control tend to thrash around and kick continuously, stirring up the bottom and shattering any coral their fins connect with. So please take a moment to adjust your weight to the minimum necessary. Dangling gauges, consoles and octopus regulators are almost guaranteed to snag on the reef, so please tuck them into your BC.

There is nothing like the pre-dive anticipation that accompanies exploring a new dive site.

Gloved divers tend to grab everything and anything, with no thought to the damage being done. Barehanded divers are much more aware of where their hands are. However, if you plan on using the NPT moorings as descent and ascent lines, you'll probably want to carry a pair of gloves in your BC pocket to protect your hands from the stinging hydroids that have colonized the ropes. But please remove the gloves when you reach the bottom, or lower your own line. Most commercial dive boats use their own weighted ascent/descent lines to avoid this problem.

Photographers are responsible for more than their fair share of reef damage. We suggest that before a photographer looks for specific subjects, he or she should locate an appropriate place to work, namely, a sandy area adjacent to the reef where it's OK to settle down on the bottom and photograph close to the reef. The upward-angle composition afforded from such a position will be reward enough. Be aware of where your fins are; their

Cuan Law, *at 105 by 45 feet (32 by 14 m), is a virtual sailing hotel for a score of lucky divers. Her size and range of activities make her perfect for non-divers as well.*

sharp edges can do a lot of damage. For close-up or macro work, if the photographer can locate a non-living handhold near the subject, he can gently grasp it with the fingertips of his free hand to help control body position and minimize contact with the living reef.

Riding turtles and chasing rays, blowing up pufferfish, and dragging shrimp and crabs from their homes is no longer acceptable behavior. You'll get more out of your interaction with the marine life if you do less bullying and chasing. Watching the fish and creatures go about their activities as if you weren't there is much more rewarding than having them flee from your approach. The slower you go, the more you'll see.

DIVING SERVICES

Dive Shops. There are no fly-by-night dive shops in the BVI. The management, instructors and staff of each facility take great pride in their professionalism and the quality of the diving they offer. The boats are generally large, seaworthy and custom designed for diving. The rental equipment is top quality and well maintained. The shops are all members (as are some of the liveaboards) of the BVI Dive Operators Association. This association works towards protecting the environment as well as ensuring that only the highest standards of safety and professionalism are adhered to.

There are three operators on Tortola (with six locations, including Cooper Island), and two on Virgin Gorda (with five locations, including Peter Island and Marina Cay). One photography/video facility in Tortola serves most of the dive shops. Anegada and Jost Van Dyke presently do not have dive operations.

Liveaboard Dive Boats. Liveaboard dive

FISH FEEDING

Scuba divers feed fishes for many reasons. It's fun to see the fishes close up, eager faces all staring into your mask. For photographers and videographers it is the easiest (and sometimes only) way to bring fishes to within close range. Some divers just assume that fish feeding is a normal diving activity, having seen pictures and videos of others doing it.

However, fish feeding is a controversial subject. Some feel it's unnatural and shows little respect for the reef inhabitants, turning them into beggars. It may also alter the normal behavioral patterns and balances on the reef. Fish feeding is probably unhealthy for the fishes. It certainly is for the diver—fishes bite.

Nonetheless, a lot of people who are otherwise fairly sensitive to the environment and respect its inhabitants do, in fact, feed fishes. We do. Here are some guidelines that make us feel better about it.

We feed fishes only at sites where it's been established, sort of like underwater petting zoos. In the BVI, the *Rhone*, the Caves and the Chimney are spots where the fishes are used to being fed.

Please don't feed them inappropriate substances. Cheezwiz is the most controversial, but in reality, anything other than their natural diet is suspect. The stingrays at Stingray City in Grand Cayman are fed only squid and ballyhoo. We use bread here in the BVI. Using anything "meatier" such as squid makes the yellowtails and others on the *Rhone* way too aggressive. However, we use a special container that controls the bread and lets only a little out at a time. Please, NO plastic bags. Divers often bring the food down in plastic bags which are torn and shredded, and left to drift in the water. Turtles and other marine life eat these bags and die.

If you feed fishes, you have to accept the fact that you're likely to be bitten. While yellowtail snappers and sergeant majors are the usual culprits, they rarely break the skin. The real danger is with "trained" green morays, barracudas and other large fishes. They're capable of inflicting serious injury, either by becoming too excited or by mistaking your soggy flesh for bait. NEVER attempt to feed sharks.

The choice is yours. If you do decide to feed the fishes, please do so responsibly.

boats in the BVI carry on the proud traditions of personal service and culinary excellence started here by charter yachts over 25 years ago. There is a competition among the crews as to who offers the best food and takes the best care of their guests. Many of them are owner-operated by couples who have made the BVI their home and will enthusiastically share their knowledge and expertise of the BVI's natural wonders. The boats range in size

Most of the dive operations offer
rendezvous diving. They will pick
you up from your yacht, take you
diving and deliver you back.

Baskin in the Sun's dive boats depart
twice daily from Prospect Reef
Resort.

from intimate two-guest sailboats to the largest trimaran in the world.

Charter Yachts (crewed). In addition to dedicated liveaboard dive boats, the BVI boasts an entire industry based on yacht chartering. There are almost 1,000 yachts available for charter, from simple bareboats to the most luxurious mega-yachts.

There are many independent (some owner-operated) crewed yachts. Some of these may offer diving, but unlike the liveaboards listed in the appendix, these are not dedicated dive boats. However, the level of service offered is overwhelming. If you've ever fantasized about "the lifestyles of the rich and famous," think about chartering a crewed yacht. The crew will pamper you with lovingly prepared mouth-watering meals and indulge your every whim as they guide you on a customized voyage through the islands.

Charter Yachts (bareboat). The majority of the boats cruising British Virgin Island waters are "bareboats"—that is, the boat is chartered without a captain or crew, a sort of "U Sail It" arrangement. Obviously, previous sailing experience is a prerequisite, but once checked-out, the yachtsmen go their own way. The popularity of bareboat chartering is due to the ease of sailing here. The winds are steady, the islands close to one another, there are virtually no hidden shoals, and there are numerous excellent anchorages. It is possible to hire a freelance captain or cook to reduce some of the responsibilities.

Enjoying diving while bareboating is easy. You can rent tanks, tank racks and whatever other scuba equipment you might need from any of the dive shops, pay the National Parks Trust mooring usage fee, study your charts, pick up a dive site mooring, and splash, you're diving. Compressors are scattered around the islands. However, diving from a sailboat can be awkward and you'll miss the local expertise and increased safety factor that diving with a commercial dive operation can add.

Rendezvous Diving. Pioneered by Underwater Safaris almost 20 years ago, the concept is very simple and very popular. A commercial dive boat with a full complement of tanks, rental gear and instructors/dive guides meets your boat, takes the divers out for one or two dives, and returns them to the boat when they're done. The dive shops take reservations over the VHF marine radio and the system works like a charm. Introductory resort courses for non-divers can be arranged the same way. Rendezvous diving is a great way for divers to get a few dives (or even a solid week's worth) without inconveniencing the non-divers on the boat or hassling with tanks and logistics.

Dive Instruction. The quality of instruction available in the BVI is excellent. Complete PADI and NAUI open water certification courses are taught at all the dive shops and on some liveaboards. Many visiting scuba-students do their pool and classroom work back home before arriving and then complete the open water portion of their training in the BVI. Such a referral program saves the student from squandering precious vacation time with academics and pool sessions. Specialty and advanced courses are also offered.

Many non-diving visitors are enticed to take the plunge and try scuba for the first time. A resort or introductory course is an excellent way to begin a diving career. While not a certification course, it is recognized and sanctioned by the certifying agencies. A brief informative lecture is followed by a shallow water familiarization session in a pool or off the beach. Then, under the direct supervision of an instructor, the beginner divers explore a coral reef or the shallow end of the *Rhone*. All this is done in half a day. The resort course graduates can then dive for the remainder of their stay—but only with an instructor and no deeper than 40 feet (12 m).

Photography Services. Rainbow Visions Photo Center (owned by the authors) is the only full service underwater photography/video facility in the BVI. It is located at Prospect Reef Resort (next to Baskin in the Sun) in Road Town and serves all of the dive companies on Tortola. Custom underwater videos on the *Rhone* are their most popular service, but photography instruction, E-6 film processing, video and still camera rentals and sales are also available. For those frustrated by less-than-spectacular results in underwater photography, the authors offer a variety of half-day advanced courses. There are also courses in housed SLR photography as well as video macro. Their new photo center includes a gallery where visitors can select and take home a framed print of an outstanding underwater scene.

CHAPTER III TORTOLA

Includes Offshore Islands

AT A GLANCE

The Sir Francis Drake Channel meanders through the British Virgin Islands like a grand boulevard for yachts. Tortola defines the north side of the channel, and the offshore islands of Norman, Peter, Salt, Cooper and Ginger line the south side, separating the Sir Francis Drake Channel from the Caribbean. Drake's Lake, as the channel is sometimes affectionately referred to, is a favorite playground for visiting yachtsmen and divers. The best and most dependable dive sites are scattered along its length.

EXPLORING TORTOLA

Tortola, the largest and most developed of the British Virgin Islands, looks somewhat like a convoluted ridge-backed lizard crawling east to west. The island is approximately 3 by 12 miles (5-19 km) long with an area of 21 square miles (54 sq km) and a population of over 13,225 (1991 census). Road Town, the Territory's capital, lies nestled deep in Road Harbour, a large beautiful natural harbour facing south toward Salt and Peter Islands.

Sage Mountain, the highest peak in the territory, climbs straight out of the sea to 1,710 feet (518 m). The steep hills of a central ridge divide Tortola into North and South Sides. Most of the island's roads run east-west, with a few thrusting straight up the hills to crest this central ridge.

Visitors usually arrive either by air at Beef Island on the East End of the island, or by ferry at Soper's Hole on the West End. The two ends are connected by Drake's Highway which runs along the south coast, bisected by Road Town in the middle.

West End. Soper's Hole, on the western tip of Tortola, is a deep harbour looking out at the US Virgins further to the west. It is usually full of boats. The ferry docks, and Customs and Immigration are on the Tortola side of the harbour. Across the water, on Frenchman's Cay, is the beautifully designed Pusser's Landing. This brightly colored, West Indian-style conglomeration of shops, restaurants, tall palm trees and marinas has become Tortola's choicest retail edifice. The Pusser's Company Store (one of four in the BVI) is the centerpiece of this delightful shopping experience. Baskin in the Sun's newly refitted dive shop in Soper's Hole is one of the most spacious and modern in the BVI. Their dive boat here often departs for the less visited north side sites.

Drake's Highway meanders out of Soper's Hole and heads east hugging the south shore. The views of St. John and Norman and Peter Islands across the channel are so serene, they're therapeutic. The coast road follows the shoreline and is fairly deserted until you reach Nanny Cay. Here you'll find a full service marina, with resort facilities, a windsurfing school, a couple of charter companies, and an assortment of shops and restaurants.

The Blue Water Divers' dive shop with their amiable instructors and fleet of dive boats has been based here for over 15 years.

Continuing on you'll pass through Sea Cow Bay, a quaint village. There are no dedicated tourist facilities here save for a few local eateries such as the Struggling Man's Place.

Road Town. Just before Road Town, you'll reach Prospect Reef Resort, home base to both Baskin in the Sun and the Rainbow Visions Photo Center. Prospect Reef is a great place to stay, especially if you're going to do a lot of

The honeycomb cowfish has horn-like spines above its eyes and a honeycomb pattern. Curious, but shy, they will generally keep a safe distance from divers.

Soper's Hole on Tortola's west end has offered safe anchorage to sailors for centuries. Today, with its Caribbean-style architecture and many fine stores, it is a popular place to visit and shop.

diving, as the rooms are very convenient to the dive shop and photo center, and it's just a short walk to all the restaurants and stores in town.

Coming into Road Town, Drake's Highway becomes Waterfront Drive and follows the edge of Road Harbour. The marinas and tourist facilities thicken. On the waterfront, across from the post office, is the ferry with its new customs and immigration facilities, where the ferries for St. Thomas and Virgin Gorda leave from, and passengers from the *Flying Cloud* and various other ships disembark. Across the street are Cell 5, Capriccio and Pusser's restaurants.

Main Street, one block back from the waterfront, is quite charming with all its shops and restaurants. Take a stroll down this narrow lane, past the old West Indian-style stores, churches and houses, as well as the soon-to-

be-retired Her Majesty's Prison, a rather bleak-looking edifice.

The inner harbour in the heart of town is almost wall-to-wall docks and marinas. On Wickhams Cay I there is the Village Cay Resort and Marina, and the Inner Harbour Marina. Behind the Social Security Building, which is home to the BVI Tourist Board, is the new and very imposing Government Administrative Building. Further back on the Cay, is the new cruise ship dock. Across the water is Wickhams Cay II, hosting the Moorings-Mariner Inn complex. Underwater Safaris is located right on the water at the Moorings-Mariner Inn, where their three dive boats serve the yachting community as well as land based divers. Treasure Isle Hotel lies in between the two Wickham Cays on Water Front Drive.

East End and Beef Island. The coast road continues east, out of town and past the old

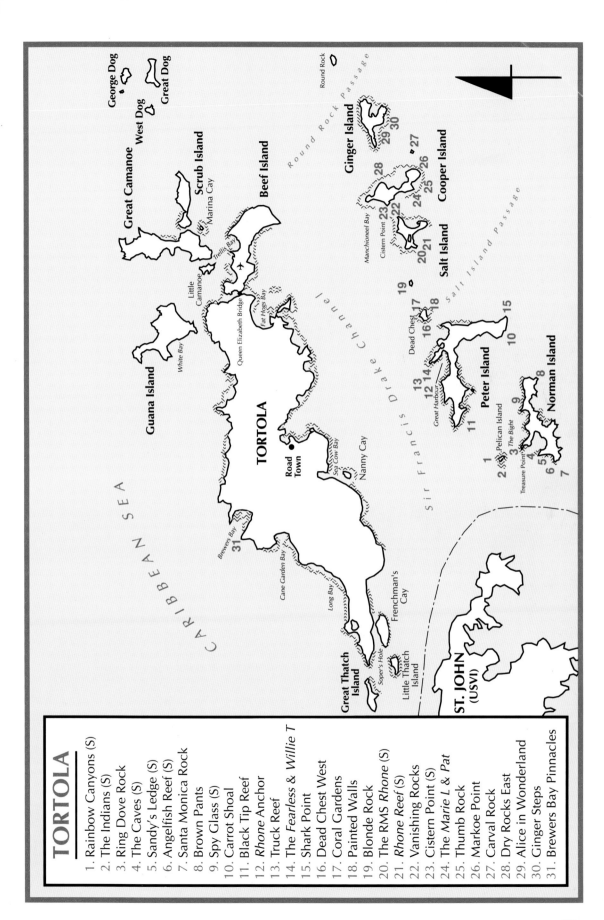

TORTOLA

1. Rainbow Canyons (S)
2. The Indians (S)
3. Ring Dove Rock
4. The Caves (S)
5. Sandy's Ledge (S)
6. Angelfish Reef (S)
7. Santa Monica Rock
8. Brown Pants
9. Spy Glass (S)
10. Carrot Shoal
11. Black Tip Reef
12. *Rhone* Anchor
13. Truck Reef
14. The *Fearless & Willie T*
15. Shark Point
16. Dead Chest West
17. Coral Gardens
18. Painted Walls
19. Blonde Rock
20. The RMS *Rhone* (S)
21. *Rhone Reef* (S)
22. Vanishing Rocks
23. Cistern Point (S)
24. The *Marie L & Pat*
25. Thumb Rock
26. Markoe Point
27. Carval Rock
28. Dry Rocks East
29. Alice in Wonderland
30. Ginger Steps
31. Brewers Bay Pinnacles

Map labels:
George Dog, West Dog, Great Dog, Round Rock, Round Rock Passage, Great Camanoe, Scrub Island, Marina Cay, Beef Island, Ginger Island, 29, 30, 27, 28, 26, 25, 24, 23, 22, Manchioneel Bay, Cistern Point, 21, 20, Cooper Island, Salt Island, Trellis Bay, Little Camanoe, Fat Hogs Bay, Queen Elizabeth Bridge, White Bay, Guana Island, Dead Chest, 19, 17, 18, 16, Salt Island Passage, 15, 13, 14, 12, Great Harbour, 10, Peter Island, TORTOLA, Road Town, Sir Francis Drake Channel, 11, Sea Cow Bay, Nanny Cay, 8, 9, Norman Island, 1, 2, Pelican Island, 3, The Bight, 4, 5, 6, 7, Treasure Point, CARIBBEAN SEA, Brewers Bay, 31, Cane Garden Bay, Long Bay, Frenchman's Cay, Soper's Hole, Great Thatch Island, Little Thatch Island, ST. JOHN (USVI)

35

CSY (now Stardust) Marina. From Road Town to East End it's called the Blackburn Highway and winds its way up and down steep hills. The view now looks up-channel, past Salt and Ginger Islands, towards Virgin Gorda. The modern H. Lavity Stout Community College in Paraquita Bay is testimony to the pace of progress in the BVI. In sheltered bays you'll pass other marina-charter boat companies; Tropic Island and Sun Yachts (as well as Blue Water Divers' new shop) in Maya Cove and Sea Breeze in Fat Hogs Bay. The terrain flattens out again as you pass through the joined tiny hamlets of Long Look, Long Swamp, Parham Town and East End. The road leads over the Queen Elizabeth toll bridge at the easternmost end of Tortola and passes over to Beef Island, where the airport and the tourist facilities (the Last Resort, Boardsailing BVI, Flukes) surrounding Trellis Bay are located. Plans calling for expansion of the airport and extensive development of Beef Island will eventually change this quiet and charming neighborhood.

The North Side. The north side of Tortola has a completely different ambiance than the more developed southern coast. Even though it faces the Atlantic Ocean, it is much more Caribbean in personality and temperament. Instead of the hustle and bustle of marinas and commerce there is the quiet timelessness of sleepy West Indian villages, deserted beaches and uninterrupted views to a distant horizon. The north side is lusher due to greater rainfall.

A good third of the north coast is virtually inaccessible except by boat or donkey trail (four wheel drive might do it). However, up along the top of the central ridge, Ridge Road winds back and forth, offering spectacular views to both the north and south. Access to Ridge Road (and the north side) is by several roads which, in a series of heart-stopping

Bomba's Shack, on Tortola's north shore, is a BVI icon, featured in magazines the world over. Rather rustic, it is a popular surfer hangout and host to notorious full-moon parties. Visitors are welcome.

Long Bay, on Tortola's north shore, is one of the most photographed beaches in the BVI. A secluded resort is tucked in among the palms and nestled into the hillside.

switchbacks, traverse up the sides of various ghuts, or ravines. From the south there is one from East End that connects with the eastern end of Ridge Road and continues down to Josiah's Bay. There are three from the Road Town area, including the famous Joe's Hill, as well as Zion Hill in the west. Many of the new roads being cut into Tortola's hills will soon also connect. On the north side, the main arteries from Ridge Road descend into Brewers Bay, Cane Garden Bay and Windy Hill, between Cane Garden and Carrot Bay.

While there is no coast road along the eastern half of the North Side, the western half does have one. The drive from Smuggler's Cove, through Long Bay, Cappoon's Bay, Apple Bay, Carrot Bay, up over Windy Hill to Cane Garden Bay and continuing on to Brewer's Bay is certainly a highlight of exploring the BVI.

The Offshore and East End Islands. The offshore islands of Norman, Peter, Salt, Cooper

and Ginger, along with their companion smaller islets and rocks, comprise the southern perimeter of the Sir Francis Drake Channel. While Tortola is big and tall enough to "catch" rain, the smaller offshore islands can't and are much more arid. These islands tend to be covered by cactus and low lying scrub.

Norman Island is the westernmost of the channel islands and the largest uninhabited island in all the BVI. Several beautiful anchorages are tucked into Norman Island's folds, but the largest and most popular is the Bight. This famous anchorage provides shelter in almost any weather and is large enough to conceal an entire flotilla—perhaps a ghost fleet of privateers. Robert Louis Stevenson is reputed to have based *Treasure Island* on Norman Island and its nefarious inhabitants. The island's namesake was a bloodthirsty pirate. He, along with Captain Kidd and Blackbeard (a.k.a. Edward (Teach) Thatch—thus all the Thatch Islands in the area), frequented these waters. Surely, they used Norman Island as a hideout, climbing Spy Glass Hill to scour the horizon, searching for heavily laden merchant ships to plunder and pillage.

Just outside the Bight is Treasure Point and its three water-level caves. The caves are a popular destination on the day-sail circuit and well worth visiting. A Tortolian family recovered a fortune in pirate treasure from the caves in the early 1900's and stories of undiscovered booty are still widely told. The shallow reef and friendly fishes surrounding Treasure Point provide perfect snorkeling. Swimming into the musty gloom of the interior of the deepest cave is a fantasy inspiring experience—is that sparkle the glint of a piece-of-eight or just the reflection off a flighty fish?

Many popular dive sites are located close to Norman Island. Several are quite protected from the prevailing weather and currents, so if you're on a boat and contemplating doing your own diving without a local guide, these are good sites.

Sailing east from Norman Island, the next major island is Peter Island, home of the famous Peter Island Yacht Club Resort. The Yacht Club offers luxurious accommodations and gourmet meals for the well heeled set. Dive BVI of Virgin Gorda operates a full service dive shop here. Their experienced and personable divemasters specialize in small groups.

Peter Island doesn't have the romantic history of Norman Island, but it does offer exquisite beaches and tranquil anchorages. Dead Man's Bay has to be one of the most photographed beaches in the Virgin Islands; its crescent shaped white sand beach fringed by palms trees and backed by steep green hills is everyone's idea of paradise. Great Harbour is where the RMS *Rhone* started her day on October 29, 1867; a hurricane intervened and she ended up on the ocean floor off Salt Island. Her massive anchor still lies at the mouth of Great Harbour—a historic dive site.

Dead Chest, as in "Yo Ho Ho, fifteen men on a dead man's chest," is a small, rugged, uninhabited island between Peter Island and Salt Island. It was purchased in the 1940's by Earl Baldwin and given to the people of the BVI, and is now part of the BVI National Park system. There are several excellent dive sites surrounding Dead Chest. Painted Walls is one of the most publicized BVI sites, but because

of its exposed location and shallow depths it is a calm weather site only.

Due to the heroism and valor they showed in rescuing the survivors of the *Rhone* over one hundred years ago, a barrel of salt is all the residents of Salt Island pay to the Crown for annual rent. Once upon a time, Salt Island was an important source of salt for Her Majesty's ships. For a fascinating glimpse of a rapidly vanishing way of life, pay a respectful visit to the Settlement. The few remaining Salt Islanders will explain their livelihood—hand-harvesting salt from the evaporative salt ponds. You can purchase conch shell trumpets and small bags of salt; this will help keep the residents viable for a little while longer. The incredible remains of the 310-foot-long (94 m) RMS *Rhone* lie just off the rocky shore of Lee Bay, Salt Island.

Manchioneel Bay on Cooper Island is another postcard-perfect beach: clear water teeming with life, yachts bobbing at anchor, powdery white sand, rows of palm trees. The services offered here are of a barefoot temperament. The Cooper Island Beach Club consists of a beach bar/restaurant—popular with the yachting crowd and several attractive bungalows available for rent. Underwater Safaris operates their very charming West Indian-style satellite facility here, complete with gingerbread eves, porch swings, full inventory and compressor.

There is excellent snorkeling and a very pretty shallow dive site right off Cistern Point on the south end of the beach, with a NPT mooring just for dinghies. Underwater Safaris runs a boat out to Cooper every morning, so day trips to this great location are easily arranged. Since Cooper Island is so centrally located, many other sites are within easy reach.

The rugged shoreline and lack of beaches or even a proper anchorage render the uninhabited Ginger Island rarely visited. Yet concealed beneath the surrounding waters are several outstanding dives.

North of Beef Island, on the eastern tip of Tortola, are several other small islands. Bellamy Cay sits in the heart of Trellis Bay and is home to the Last Resort restaurant and cabaret. Uninhabited Scrub Island is rather inhospitable, with a steep ridge rising quickly from the sea and few beaches. A newly cut road proclaims future development. Scrub does, however, provide a measure of protection for Marina Cay, the long established yachting facility located on an impressive reef and recently taken over by Pusser's. Great Camanoe is occupied by a handful of private houses and rental holiday homes. Guana Island, so named because of the resemblance of a rock formation to the head of an iguana, is home to the exclusive Guana Island Club. White Bay, the site of the Club, is one of the most spectacular beaches in the BVI.

Where To Stay

The options are varied and wonderful: resorts, hotels, small inns and holiday homes. Many first time visitors elect to stay in one of the better known hotels, and then during their holiday search out a smaller, more personable inn or rental house for subsequent trips. There are roughly 20 hotels and over 40 guest houses located on the islands covered in this chapter.

There are a few major hotel/resorts on Tortola: Long Bay Beach Resort, the Moorings-Mariner Inn, Prospect Reef Resort, and Peter Island Resort & Yacht Harbour (on Peter Island) are the biggest. Prospect Reef (Baskin in the Sun), Peter Island (Dive BVI), the Moorings (Underwater Safaris), Nanny Cay (Blue Water Divers) and Cooper Island Beach Club (Underwater Safaris) are especially convenient if you plan on doing a lot of diving as the respective dive companies' boats depart directly from the dock. Other hotels in and around Road Town include Treasure Isle Hotel (across from the Moorings), Fort Burt, Maria's by the Sea and Sea View Hotel.

If you want to stay on a beach, you'll have to stay on the north side. If you want to dive, you'll probably have to rent a car as the dive shops are all on the south side. Cane Garden is the most popular beach with lots of small guest cottages and inns. The Ole Works Inn is clean and affordable, and right next to the beach. Brewers Bay is the site of the only official campground on Tortola. Sugar Mill Hotel, on Little Apple Bay, is a highly rated hotel with great atmosphere, fantastic food and a beach of sorts. Sebastian's, on Apple Bay, is nice and affordable and on the beach. Long Bay Beach Resort is elegant and spread out along scenic Long Bay Beach. Fort Recovery Villas and Frenchman's Cay Hotel are on the south side and have small beaches. Rental houses run the gamut from clean and simple to expensive but-man-what-a-place-I-can't-get-over-that-view.

Eat, Drink And Be Merry

The dining and night life scene here is not one of big resort-style restaurants and floor show night clubs. Most of the night life centers around local bands playing at various restaurant/night spots. That is, if you still have enough energy left after a full day playing in the sun, sea and sand to go out and party. Those at sea usually end up lying on the deck of their boat, staring up at the stars wondering why every day doesn't end like this.

However, if you just must go out and "get down," try the Paradise Pub in Road Town, the Jolly Roger at West End, Tamarind over in Josiah's Bay or Quito's at Cane Garden Bay. If you're on Tortola during the proper lunar phase, check out Bomba's Shack for the notorious Full Moon Party held every month. The Last Resort and Tony Snell's cabaret show is a must-see for those chartering; his inside jokes and songs will bring tears of laughter to your eyes. Some of the hotels and other restaurants also host live bands, especially on weekends in season—just ask around.

The official tourist guide, the *Welcome* magazine, lists over 60 restaurants on Tortola alone. We can't possibly compete with that compendium, but instead offer a short list of some of our favorites. They run the gamut from cheap and local, to cheap and American, and on to expensive-but-good-by-any-standard. Most of these are independent and not part of a major hotel. Part of the joy of visiting the BVI is the variety of dining experiences available. So get out of your hotel or guest house, or dinghy ashore from your yacht and eat around.

Around Road Town. Some of our, and the local divemasters', favorites are C&F (great ribs and sea food), Spaghetti Junction (fine Italian cuisine), Virgin Queen (renowned for their pizza), Capriccio (sidewalk cafe) and Inside the Fish Trap (good burgers and Sunday prime rib). Also popular are the Paradise Pub, the air-conditioned Pusser's Outpost & Deli, The Captain's Table, and Santa Maria. They all offer a gratifying dining experience for the hungry but discriminating diver/diner. For more of a local West Indian flavor (and generally cheaper fare) try the Roti Palace, Maria's by the Sea, Marlene's, M&S Pastry and

Cell 5 Lounge. The following offer fine dining along with their rooms: Fort Burt, Treasure Isle Hotel, the Moorings-Mariner Inn and Prospect Reef Resort (Upstairs Restaurant and the Scuttlebutt Bar & Grill) .

Outside Town. Peg Leg Landing in Nanny Cay is popular with the sailing-diving-partying crowd. Pusser's Landing in Soper's Hole offers open-air dockside dining as well as a fine restaurant upstairs. Great for a casual lunch on the beach, or dinner and dancing with a steel-band are Rhymer's, Quito's Gazebo, Stanley's (home to the tire swing of Jimmy Buffet fame) and Myett's on Cane Garden Bay. Quito writes and performs his own West Indian folk music. A BVI institution is Bomba's Shack on the beach at Apple Bay. Mrs. Scattliffe's in Carrot Bay promises exotic local fare along with entertainment provided by her family. For an authentic island experience try the bush tea at the North Shore Shell Museum, also in Carrot Bay. Frenchman's Cay, the Jolly Roger, Sebastian's On The Beach and The Apple are all good restaurants, all with their own individual style.

Brandywine Bay, Long Bay Beach Resort, the Sugar Mill and the Tamarind Club are considered to be four of the top restaurants on Tortola. The chefs at Peter Island Yacht Club also garner enthusiastic praise.

Almost everyone stops at Sky World, located high on the Ridge Road. In addition to fine food and outrageous blender drinks, the view from their observation deck takes in almost 360 degrees; from Anegada and St. Croix (when it's clear) to Virgin Gorda, the offshore islands, Jost Van Dyke and St Thomas. Don't miss it—sunsets are a special treat. De Loose Mongoose and Conch Shell Point Restaurant are in Trellis Bay. The Cooper Island Beach Club, Marina Cay and the *Willie T II* (anchored off Norman Island) serve the yachting crowd.

WHAT TO DO

Touring. Tortola offers a lot more than only diving. Renting a car and setting out to explore the island is a favorite pastime. Since the roads, and drivers too for that matter, can be a bit overwhelming, the more timid motorist might be better off hiring a car and driver for the day—this has the added benefit of sampling all those blender drinks not quite suicidal. The stories and local knowledge your driver will share make this a special treat.

While in Road Town make sure you visit the J.R. O'Neal Botanic Gardens. This little treasure is tucked into the back of Road Town, across from the police station. A quiet and peaceful retreat, the four-acre (1.6 ha) garden boasts representative flora from different climatic zones, including seaside, arid and rain forest. Learn to identify some of the beautiful tropical flowers you've been admiring.

Stradling the highest point in the Territory at 1,710 feet (518 m), Sage Mountain National Park preserves the remnants of the hardwood forests that once carpeted much of these islands. While not a true rainforest (it's not quite wet enough) Sage Mountain certainly feels like one. Neatly laid out gravel trails will lead you past large elephant ears, huge philodendrons and beneath a vine-laden canopy of mahogany, cedar and kapok trees. Hiking these trails is a cool and refreshing break from diving and beaches. Don't miss the prehistoric-looking tree ferns and the incredible views of Tortola and the outlying islands.

Shopping. In Road Town most of the tourist oriented stores are located on Main Street, that charming narrow lane that parallels Waterfront Drive. Esme's Shop, located in the Square in front of the post office, sells cold drinks and, more importantly, current U.S. newspapers.

There are a handful of stores that everyone recommends when gift shopping for the folks back home. In addition to being located in a very photogenic gingerbread-style house, Sunny Caribbee Herb and Spice Company, sells beautifully packaged jars and baskets of herbs and spices with all sorts of clever mixes, such as "love potion" and "hangover cure." Pusser's Company Store has a wide selection of souvenirs and a nice line of clothing. Their stores are so full of nautical knick-knacks it is almost like visiting a museum.

Ooh La La, Carol's Gift Shop, Collector's Corner and Little Denmark have gifts as well. Island wear, both funky and elegant, can be found at Serendipity, Castaways, the Shirt Shack, Violets (for lingerie), Caribbean Handprints and Kids in De Sun. For more utilitarian needs check out Bolos (batteries, film processing, music, etc.), KIS (film & processing) and J.R. O'Neal Ltd. (drugstore). The supermarkets include Riteway and KB's. Beer and booze can be purchased at the supermarkets as wells as Ticos (two locations).

Outside of town make sure you visit Soper's Hole in West End. This shopping complex is an example of development done right. All the shops are designed in the traditional West Indian style and painted bright pastel colors. The centerpiece is Pusser's Landing, with two restaurants and a Company Store. There is also a Baskin in the Sun dive shop, Island Treasures (Caribbean art, books and gifts) Zenaida's (exotic jewelry and clothing) and Sea Urchin (T-shirts and beach wear). At the opposite end of Tortola, at Trellis Bay on Beef Island are a few stores including Flukes (gift shop and gallery). Don't forget to stop by the authors' Photo Center and Gallery at Prospect Reef Resort for framed and unframed photographic prints.

All the dive shops sell a wide variety of necessary and souvenir items, in addition to competitively priced dive equipment. Of course, there are many more shopping experiences than we can list, so we've saved a few treasures for you to discover on your own.

Beaches. Virtually all of Tortola's beaches are on the north side. The most popular is Cane Garden Bay. This picture-postcard perfect beach comes complete with a long expanse of white sand, tall majestic palm trees, sheltered waters and sail boats bobbing at anchor. Stanley's Welcome Bar dates back to the Jimmy Buffet days of "cheeseburger in paradise." The tire swing out front epitomizes the laziness and carefree feeling of a day spent doing nothing on a beach in the West Indies. There are several other bar/restaurants on the beach as well as a simple hotel and numerous guest houses.

Tucked into a deep bay just to the east is Brewer's Bay, a much less developed beach area. Brewer's Bay is home to Tortola's only campground, a small but charming beach bar and some very good snorkeling. In the winter watch out for large swells and strong currents out at the points surrounding the bay.

To the west of Cane Garden Bay, on the other side of precipitous Windy Hill, is the town of Carrot Bay. There's not really a beach here, but the village is very much a sleepy West Indian fishing village. Continuing west is Apple Bay, the most popular surfing beach. In the winter when there's a storm in the North Atlantic, and the big waves—occasionally over 10 feet (3 m)—roll in, the surfers gather here. On calmer days it is a beautiful beach for swimming and body surfing. Bomba's Shack and Sebastian's are the beach-front establishments.

Continuing west, you crest a hill and then look down upon one of Tortola's most famous views: Long Bay Beach stretching out to the isolated peak of Belmont Point. The Long Bay Beach Resort and several guest houses are on the near end of the beach; further down it's a little more private. There's no snorkeling here, but the sea is wonderfully refreshing to swim in. As with the other north side beaches, be careful of large winter waves. Following a rough road west from Long Bay, you'll come to remote Smuggler's Cove, a smaller protected bay offering reasonable snorkeling.

There are several accessible East End beaches. The views of Josiah's Bay from the Ridge Road are especially inviting, and the beach is simply beautiful. Elizabeth Beach and Little (Elizabeth) Bay are slightly more difficult

While there still are no traffic lights in the territory, the Queen Elizabeth Bridge, joining Tortola and Beef Island (site of the airport) requires a toll to pass.

to get to, but the jolting trek over a rugged dirt road is worth it. They are deserted beaches with very few visitors. On Beef Island is another Long Bay, this one just over the Queen Elizabeth Bridge, at the base of Little Mountain.

Most of the offshore islands are laden with beaches. Ferries go to Jost Van Dyke, Peter Island and Cooper Island. The day trips listed below go to some of the hot popular islands as well.

Activities and Day Trips. In addition to exploring Tortola's sights and beaches, there is an abundance of other activities to partake in. Most popular is day sailing. This is an ideal way for the shore-based visitor to spend a day out on the water exploring other islands. The boats all offer some variation on the sailing, snorkeling, island hopping, lunch and rum drink theme, usually heading out to the Caves or the Baths. If you just want to go snorkeling, Caribbean Images's power boat provides a less expensive alternative. Powerboat rentals are available for those who want to chart their own island hopping. There is a glass bottom boat plying these waters as well as faster run-abouts. Sport fishing and even kayak rentals are available.

Instruction in windsurfing (Boardsailing BVI), underwater photography and video (Rainbow Visions), sailing (Offshore Sailing School) and of course, diving (the various dive shops) are all available. Furthermore, there's horseback riding (Mr. Thomas and Shadow), tennis (various resorts), and pitch and putt golf (Prospect Reef Resort).

DIVING AND DIVE SHOPS

The majority of diving in the BVI occurs around the islands described in this chapter. While there are lots of Virgin Gorda sites and a half dozen or so near Jost Van Dyke, the most dependable and regularly visited sites are located along the five islands that make up the southern border of the Sir Francis Drake Channel: Norman, Peter, Salt, Cooper and Ginger Islands. These islands offer a tremendous variety in both topography and required skill level. No matter what the weather conditions, there is always a sheltered site to be found. On calm days the offshore pinnacles beckon with promises of extraordinary dives.

There are very few dives off Tortola itself. On occasion, visitors have gone shore diving in front of Prospect Reef Resort, but basically there is no diving along Tortola's south coast. On the north coast, there are some sites around Brewer's Bay, but these are boat dives. Desperate to get wet cheaply, divers have gone in at Cane Garden Bay and Smuggler's Cove, but it's hardly worth it. The east side of Brewer's Bay is a better shore dive, but access is difficult because of private property preventing entry near the site.

The addresses and phone numbers of the following shops are listed in the appendix.

Baskin in the Sun

Prospect Reef Resort and Soper's Hole

Baskin in the Sun is the largest dive company in Tortola with facilities at Prospect Reef Resort and Soper's Hole. Their shops are particularly well stocked with diving equipment and accessories. The operation prides itself on offering top quality, personable service. Specializing in week-long dive packages, this people-pleasing enterprise lures divers back year after year.

The West End operation in Soper's Hole takes advantage of calm days and heads out to the lesser-dived sites around Jost Van Dyke and Tortola's north shore.

In addition to the regular scuba instruction, from introductory up to divemaster, Baskin in the Sun instructors love to teach specialty courses. Their favorites are Caribbean reef ecology and fish identification. For guests at Prospect Reef the introductory resort course starts in the Olympic-sized pool. Unlimited diving packages are offered in conjunction with Prospect Reef Resort and Long Bay Beach Resort. While rendezvous diving is not their specialty, Baskin in the Sun will meet boats at various anchorages.

Baskin in the Sun often runs all-day trips in addition to regularly scheduled night dives, especially when there's a dive group. These trips may be to the *Chikuzen*, or the Dogs and the Baths.

With the Rainbow Visions Photo Center right on the premises at Prospect Reef Resort, it is very easy to rent still and video camera equipment, take a photo course or star in your own custom video.

Blue Water Divers

Nanny Cay and Hodge's Creek

Blue Water Divers is the oldest owner-operated dive shop on Tortola. They have several boats, but their pride and joy is *Cat B'lue*, a very stable 47-foot catamaran. *Cat B'lue* is roomy enough for 30 divers, but they usually limit it to half that number. Blue Water Divers plans only one two-dive trip each day, so their departure time and schedule are very relaxed—simpatico with a laid back Caribbean vacation.

Their main facility is located at Nanny Cay Resort, just a few miles west of Road Town. Blue Water Divers offers hotel-dive packages through Nanny Cay.

They have dive equipment for rent and provide rendezvous diving for many of the islands' charter companies. Underwater photography and video services are provided by Rainbow Visions.

Blue Water Divers has recently opened a dive shop at the new Hodges Creek Marina in Maya Cove. This location is closer to the *Rhone* and especially convenient for East End residents and charterers from Tropic Isle, Sea Breeze and Sun Yachts.

Dive BVI

Peter Island and Marina Cay

Strictly speaking Dive BVI is a Virgin Gorda operation, but their satellite facilities on Peter Island and Marina Cay deserve mention here. Located at the Peter Island Yacht Club and Marina on Peter Island, this dive shop specializes in small groups. While most of their clients are guests in the Amway-owned hotel, they will take divers who come out to the island by ferry or who are on sailboats nearby. Due to their location on the south side of the Sir Francis Drake Channel, the Peter Island shop is only a few minutes from many dive sites. By request, Rainbow Visions videographers will come along and produce custom videotapes of visitor's dives.

Underwater Safaris

The Moorings and Cooper Island

Underwater Safaris, headquartered at The Moorings on Wickhams Cay II in Road Town, pioneered "rendezvous diving" almost 20 years ago. A simple call on the VHF marine radio or, these days, the cellular phone, is all it takes to make a reservation. A fully equipped dive boat will come out to the anchorage, rendezvous with the charter boat, and take the certified divers diving, give the scuba-wannabes a PADI introductory course, or even do referral openwater dives. They'll rendezvous anywhere from Norman Island to the Dogs.

As with all the shops in the BVI, they offer instruction from introductory up to divemaster. Underwater Safaris maintains a large inventory of rental equipment. The dive shop will even deliver full tanks to your boat and cart the empties away. They work with the Rainbow Visions Photo Center to provide photo-video services to their clients.

Underwater Safaris also operates a full service facility at Cooper Island. Their Cooper Island shop, tucked in the palms just off the beach, is a charming West Indian cottage, complete with porch and porch swings, peaked roof, gingerbread trim and pretty garden. At least one of their dive boats stops at Cooper every morning so you can always get a ride out there.

Rainbow Visions

Underwater Photography

Owned by the authors, the Rainbow Visions Photo Center is the largest underwater photography facility in the Virgin Islands. They provide photo services to most of the local dive companies. The most popular product is a custom video of a visitor's *Rhone* dives, complete with opening credits, topside footage and underwater filming on two dives. Pretty much any time there is a dive boat going to the wreck of the *Rhone* there's a Rainbow Visions videographer on board.

The Photo Center, located next to Baskin in the Sun at Prospect Reef Resort, offers E-6 film processing, camera and video rentals and sales, personalized instruction, and in their gallery a wide selection of beautiful photographs. From half-day introductory photo/video classes to two-day PADI specialty courses to advanced classes in housed autofocus SLR photography and macro video, the emphasis is on fun, results and personal in-water instruction.

Liveaboard Dive Boats

Because most BVI liveaboards are based out of Tortola, they are being listed here. Many other boats offer diving, either on board or via rendezvous diving with one of the shops, but the ones listed here are the established liveaboards, though not all offer diving as the predominant activity.

Cuan Law

For those who prefer the convenience of liveaboard diving but don't want to give up the luxury of a fine hotel, book a week-long charter on Trimarine's huge *Cuan Law*. This 105-foot (32 m) sailing trimaran offers ten double staterooms, each with a private head and shower. All cabins are on the main deck and open directly into the huge main salon. Unlike many boats, *Cuan Law* has many places where you can be by yourself, and the massive top deck has two hammocks along with enough space to play volleyball!

This liveaboard, with all its comforts and

The Indians and Pelican Island are popular destinations for divers and snorkelers. The shallow reefs surrounding them are healthy and full of fishes.

activities, is perfect for non-diving companions. Meals are served on the covered aft deck. Dinners, especially, are gourmet affairs. Fast and stable inflatable dinghies with good ladders for diving are always ready to take you on a shore excursion.

While *Cuan Law* doesn't offer four or five dives a day like some gorilla liveaboards do, their three dives a day, when combined with all the other activities and island exploration, seem to satisfy even the most hard-core diver. Owners Annie and Duncan Muirhead have been running liveaboards for over 20 years and know how to do it right. And nothing beats the sense of exhilaration when the crew hoists canvas and *Cuan Law* surges forward under full sail.

Promenade

Multi-hulls make great liveaboards. They're stable, have plenty of deck space for dive gear and suiting up, and you get to sail from dive site to dive site. The 65-foot (20 m) *Promenade* has all that, plus the level of comfort and attention of a top quality charter yacht. A well maintained owner-operated vessel, David and Fiona Dugdale's *Promenade* enjoys an

Overwhelmed, the protective father of this patch of ripe sergeant major eggs has been temporarily driven off. A rock beauty takes advantage of the lapse to gorge on fresh caviar.

excellent reputation with charter brokers. She takes a maximum of ten guests.

Gypsy Wind

The 47-foot (14 m) *Gypsy Wind* is owner-operated by Clive Petrovic and Amanda Baker. This sloop-rigged sailboat takes only two people, but offers the most personal service you can imagine. It's a great honeymoon charter. While *Gypsy Wind* does have an onboard compressor, there are enough tanks onboard and enough fill stations around that they usually don't use it. True gourmet fare is painstakingly prepared by Amanda. Clive, a marine biologist, loves to heighten his guests' appreciation of the underwater world.

Wanderlust

According to owner Dick Nichol, *Wanderlust* is the boat for wimp divers. Even though the 65-foot (20 m) trimaran has all the trappings for diving (compressor, tanks, unlimited dive gear, two instructor/guides) they specialize in a "low volume" diving vacation with luxury accommodations and exquisite service. Catering to an upscale clientele interested in only a dive or two a day, *Wanderlust* provides easy no-hassle diving. The crew of six offers so many other activities that diving is almost a secondary pastime. Guests who have never

considered scuba before are often enticed into trying an introductory course. Large and roomy throughout, *Wanderlust* accommodates up to 12 guests in elegant luxury.

Encore

Another trimaran, 53-foot (16 m) *Encore* takes a maximum of eight guests, though they like to limit it to just four divers and one dive a day.

DIVE SITES

Pelican Island

1. RAINBOW CANYONS (S)

DEPTH:	25-60 FEET
	(8-18 M)
LEVEL:	NOVICE
ACCESS:	BOAT
ANCHORAGE:	PELICAN;
	THE BIGHT

Rainbow Canyons is a wonderful site for new divers and those looking to get their fins wet for the first time after a hiatus. Located on the southwest corner of uninhabited Pelican

Island, this lee-side dive offers conservative depths, a variety of habitats and good snorkeling in the shallows. Select the mooring furthest to the south. Under the mooring you'll find big coral heads where squadrons of parrotfishes nibble away at the coral, and iridescent blue lettuce sea slugs, though common, are well camouflaged. As you swim away from shore, the coral heads coalesce into a classic spur-and-groove formation, with coral ridges radiating out from shore separated by narrow sand canyons. It's great fun to mosey down one of these canyons looking for spotted drums, sharpnose puffers, crinoids and flame scallops in the hidden recesses.

At a depth of 50 to 60 feet (15-18 m), the coral ridges end and only scattered oases of small coral formations continue out into the sand. Taking the time to completely inventory one of these reef microcosms can be very rewarding. Also look for garden eels poking their heads out of the sand, weaving back and forth to some subsea rhythm. Continue south along the reef edge, intercepting schools of creole wrasse sweeping down from mid-water to be cleaned by juvenile Spanish hogfish. Just before the point there is a sharply defined canyon that cuts back along the shoreline. In the summer months this area is often teeming with thousands of bait fish. Large majestic tarpon slice through these schools like rapiers through silk.

Nearby, a couple of hundred yards to the north, is another NPT mooring. It marks a site called Pelican Island, which is, as you might imagine, similar to Rainbow Canyons.

2. THE INDIANS (S)

DEPTH:	10-50 FEET
	(3-15 M)
LEVEL:	NOVICE
ACCESS:	BOAT
ANCHORAGE:	THE INDIANS

The Indians is justifiably one of the most popular dive sites in the BVI. It's shallow, easy to find, generally calm, offers great snorkeling and has beautiful corals and plentiful fishes. Just west of Pelican Island, four jagged rock

pinnacles protrude 50 feet (15 m) above the sea. It's problematic whether they were named the Indians because they look like feathers in a headdress, or maybe teepees, or even old wooden cigar store Indians. Whatever the reason, they're a great dive.

There are numerous moorings on the Indians, but whichever you pick up, the basic dive plan is to circumnavigate the pinnacles. As your maximum depth is 50 feet (15 m)— most of the dive is spent in less than 30 feet (9 m)—your air should last the fifty or so minutes required for a leisurely tour around the rocks and back to your boat.

Starting your dive from the northernmost (white) dive mooring on the west side, swim to the rocks and turn right at the wall (proceeding counterclockwise). Swimming along the base of the cliff with the wall to your left, you'll pass over an area of healthy corals undercut with crevices and sponge-laden ledges. A little further along, the "sunken Indian" will appear on your right and you'll pass through a steep-walled canyon. There is a very active cleaning station up on the southern end of the sunken Indian, serving mostly creole wrasse and bar jacks. Rounding the southernmost Indian you'll encounter an area of abundant large coral

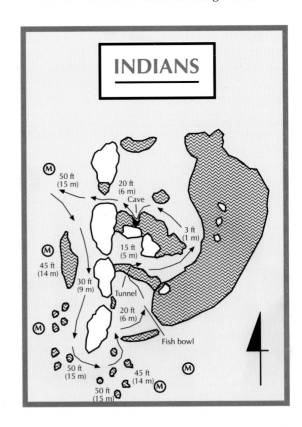

INDIANS

Guided snorkel tours are available for those non-divers interested in learning more about the undersea world. Several different sites are usually visited on an outing.

heads with profuse fish life including aloof schoolmaster snapper, bold parrotfishes and charming trunkfishes. As you continue up the far side, still keeping the rock formation to your left, you'll have to swim up and over a brain and elkhorn coral-lined ridge and down into the "fish bowl", a shallow bowl that is often filled to overflowing with bait fish, especially in summer. Here you can watch the great drama of life in the sea unfold as jacks, snappers and even lizardfishes cut through the schools of fry, and pelicans dive bomb from above.

On the far side of the "fish bowl" there is a narrow tunnel that leads into a smaller bowl. After passing through it, bear right until the bottom almost reaches the surface and then turn left back towards the pinnacle. Schools of blue tang meander around these shallows looking for tasty algae to graze on. Feisty damselfishes attempt to chase them (and visiting divers) with a well placed nip. Sticky sun anemones, along with their associated shrimps, carpet the rocky walls here. Just before you reach the wall there is a fascinating cave, complete with a skylight, on your left. As it is small and has a silty bottom we recommend that only two divers at a time venture inside and avoid using your fins. Watching the resident school of glassy sweepers cavort in the spotlight is a mesmerizing experience. Shoot plenty of film, but hold back on your strobe power as these highly reflective fish tend to "burn out." Exiting the cave you can either swim through a shallow narrow pass between two of the

The shallow reefs at the Indians are darkened by swirling clouds of bait fish in the summer. Sleek tarpon, jacks and even lizardfish prey on this movable feast.

Indians and take a short cut back to your boat, or you can continue around and complete your circumnavigation. While it is possible to circle the Indians on one dive, it would take several visits to fully appreciate all the coral beauty and fish diversity this site offers.

Snorkeling. The whole east side, being so shallow, is especially good for snorkeling, as long as strong winds don't kick up the seas.

Norman Island

3. RING DOVE ROCK

DEPTH:	15-70 FEET
	(5-21 M)
LEVEL:	NOVICE TO
	INTERMEDIATE
ACCESS:	BOAT
ANCHORAGE:	THE BIGHT

While Santa Monica Rock may be a wilderness sea mount out in open sea, Ring Dove Rock is a fertile garden of a sea mount hidden in plain sight. Located in front of Norman Island's Bight, on a line between Treasure Point and Pelican Island, many charterers sail over this site unaware of the beauty that lies directly beneath their keels. With the installation of the NPT moorings, Ring Dove has become a lot easier to find.

Picking up the mooring will, under normal sea conditions, place your boat along the northern side of the pinnacle. Directly below is a sandy area in 55 feet (17 m) of water which is an excellent place to start the dive. Spiraling up and around the formation (we recommend a counter clockwise rotation) you'll swim over a sloping bottom well covered by gorgonians and healthy sea fans. There are many rocky coral heads that stand up off the bottom, whose bases and sides are undercut and honeycombed. Lurking in these coral condos are lobsters, shy juvenile angelfishes, and small moray eels.

Coming around the far side of the pinnacle you'll see the thick cloud of sergeant majors always feeding in the current over the top of the rock. Two sand canyons cut through the summit. Crinoids, beautiful encrusting sponges, and lacy gorgonians line their walls. The sandy bottom is pockmarked by the dens of yellowhead jawfish, as well as furrowed by the slow meandering paths of burrowing red heart urchins, upon whose bellies can be found the tiny white heart urchin crab.

Overall this is a very busy reef, with clouds of plankton-eaters foraging in the water column above the rock, parrotfishes and trumpetfish roaming through the velvety gorgonians, and the bottom lit with splashes of color from iridescent purple tunicates and bright golden zoanthids on red rope sponge. Gangs of butterflyfishes often follow divers around, waiting for them to inadvertently chase sergeant majors away from the purple

A stoplight parrotfish grazes on living coral with its fused beak-like teeth. It extracts the nutrients and excretes the ground-up limestone in great silty clouds.

egg patches they were guarding. The butterflyfishes then charge in as a group and feast on sergeant major caviar. The butterflyfishes are so fearless while they gorge that photographers can place the extension tube framers of their Nikonos cameras right into the melee and get great close-up shots of the fish. Rock beauties, slender filefishes and well-fed lizardfishes round out the population.

Caution. There is one significant hazard here, in addition to occasionally strong currents, and that is the amount of boat traffic overhead. Because the top of Ring Dove is so shallow and sailboats don't make any noise as their deep keels cruise by, it is vitally important to surface only at your boat and to prominently display a large dive flag.

4. THE CAVES (S)

DEPTH:	5-40 FEET
	(1.5-12 M)
LEVEL:	NOVICE
ACCESS:	BOAT
ANCHORAGE:	THE BIGHT

The Caves is one of the most popular day sail and charter boat destinations in the BVI and justifiable so. It's calm and clear, has lots of friendly fishes, and boasts a fascinating history with the allure of buried pirate treasure. While more of a snorkel site than a dive site, it certainly is worth visiting, if only for a between-dive snorkel.

Located just around the corner from the Bight (one of the most popular anchorages in the BVI), the Caves consist of three water-level caves that penetrate back into aptly named Treasure Point. It is here, legend has it, that a Tortola family recovered a fortune in pirate treasure at the turn of the century. Dinghy over from the Bight or pick up one of the NPT moorings; be aware of possible backwinding and watch out for lots of swimmers.

The most spectacular cave is the left-hand or northernmost one. A set of submerged rock platforms lie in the entrance and then the cave sweeps to the right, penetrating 70 or so musky feet (21 m) back into the hillside. Bring a dive light to illuminate the way. Cup corals, sponges and shrimp line the walls underwater. You can stand up once you're inside a bit. That glint in the furthest recess just might be a Spanish doubloon. The southernmost cave faces directly out to sea and many an intrepid photographer has tried to frame a sailboat in the peaked entrance.

Outside the caves, the wall drops 40 feet (12 m) to a sloping sandy bottom. Hordes of sergeant majors patrol, looking for snorkelers brave enough to bring a bread handout. Parrotfishes and yellowtail snappers will then move in to pick up the scraps. If there's no surge (usually there isn't) swim right up to the cliff face for a close examination of the marine life. For the non-diver this is a perfect

Looking remarkably like a piece of ordinary sponge, the longlure frogfish can hide in plain sight. The frogfish attracts unsuspecting fishes by twitching its natural lure. When a fish gets close enough the frogfish lunges forward and inhales it whole, on occasion swallowing a fish longer than itself.

opportunity to get up close and personal with Christmas tree worms, little gobies and blennies, damselfishes and even fire coral (note the stinging hairs).

If you are an avid snorkeler, you may want to continue on to Privateer Bay to the south. Swim over the sea grass beds looking for turtles, rays and barracudas. Tucked into the bay are a series of shallow ledges worth investigating. That site is known as "Sandy's," and is explored on scuba as an introductory or "critter" dive.

5. SANDY'S LEDGE (S)

DEPTH:	5-40 FEET
	(1.5-12 M)
LEVEL:	NOVICE
ACCESS:	BOAT
ANCHORAGE:	THE BIGHT;
	THE CAVES

Between the Caves and Angelfish Reef lies a shallow bay. Privateer Bay was ignored for years because a coral ledge prevents access to the rocky beach. However, it's this shallow coral ledge that is now entertaining divers for hours at a time. This is a superb "critter dive." Until a mooring is placed here, the best bet is to leave your boat moored at the Caves or in the Bight and come over by dinghy. Set your dinghy anchor in the eel grass and make sure that it is securely dug in.

There are four parallel ecosystems to explore. The undercut ledge itself, the rock rubble at its base, a sand strip and the eel grass bed with its mini-coral heads. Start your dive with an extremely leisurely tour along the coral ledge. You can't miss it. The top of the ledge is in about six feet (2 m) of water. Lots and lots of juvenile fishes shelter here; look for grunts, baby queen angels and yellow-phase blue tangs. Divers with skilled eyes can find longlure frogfish and scorpionfish. Easier to spot are banded coral shrimp and lima fileclams (flame scallops). As you work your way along the ledge, inspect the rounded rocks at your feet and the sand strip behind you. Both areas are full of life and they form a natural corridor along which lots of fishes travel.

The eel grass further back is worthy of exploration. Eagle rays and turtles are often spotted cruising by. But the real treat here is the opportunity to get down on your belly and move in close to the low-lying desk-sized coral formations that are scattered about. These mini-oases attract hordes of tiny fishes. Because there is no place for them to go they won't flee, and you can get an intimate view of them and their habitat.

With perennially calm conditions and very shallow depths, this is a dive for everyone.

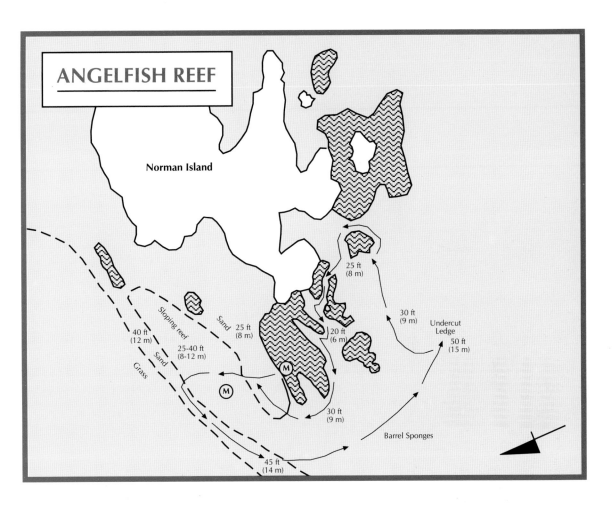

ANGELFISH REEF

Norman Island

25 ft (8 m)

30 ft (9 m)

Undercut Ledge

50 ft (15 m)

Sloping reef

Sand

40 ft (12 m)

25 ft (8 m)

25-40 ft (8-12 m)

Sand

20 ft (6 m)

Grass

M

M

30 ft (9 m)

Barrel Sponges

45 ft (14 m)

6. ANGELFISH REEF (S)

DEPTH:	20-65 FEET
	(6-20 M)
LEVEL:	NOVICE TO
	INTERMEDIATE
ACCESS:	BOAT
ANCHORAGE:	THE BIGHT;
	PRIVATEER BAY
SNORKELING:	ADVANCED ONLY

The southwestern tip of Norman Island is a rocky wave-swept point that continues underwater as a series of high ridges and a maze of canyons. Of the two NPT moorings on the lee side of the point, choose the deeper one and be aware of wind shifts. Below are two sand strips that parallel the ridge. The shallower one is in 25 feet (8 m) of water and

is a great place to finish your dive while watching the yellowhead jawfish, sand tilefish, goatfishes and sailfin blennies eke out their existence in the sand. Swimming down the slope to the deeper sand channel, be on the lookout for trumpetfish, parrotfishes and, of course, angelfishes. Following the sand path you might spot large stingrays, a mixed school of French and smallmouth grunts, swirling schools of sennet, conch out in the eel grass, and maybe even a gold-spotted snake eel. Up the slope to your left is a field of good sized barrel sponges.

When you reach a tall undercut ledge filled with grunts and blackbar soldierfish, it's time to turn left and head back up the slope, though now you're on the other side of the point. If you still have plenty of air, continue on up to the shallows and there you'll find a rocky coral head that is teeming with fish life; the grunts, snappers and wrasses are so thick that they obscure the coral behind them. Now it's time to try to find the one narrow canyon that will lead back through the rocky point to the dive

Though the 4-inch (10 cm) sharpnose puffer lacks the size and spines of some of its larger cousins, it still is capable of inflating.

boat. As you work your way through this maze, look along the bottom for spotted drums and soapfishes lurking under little ledges. Up towards the surface, keep an eye out for schools of palometa swimming through the underwater surf formed by the waves breaking on the rocks.

7. SANTA MONICA ROCK

DEPTH:	20-70 FEET
	(6-21 M)
LEVEL:	INTERMEDIATE
	TO ADVANCED
ACCESS:	BOAT
ANCHORAGE:	THE BIGHT;
	PRIVATEER BAY

Santa Monica Rock is one of those sites that the local divemasters truly look forward to diving. Located in open water, three-quarters of a mile (1.2 km) southwest of Angelfish Reef on Norman Island, Santa Monica Rock is an underwater pinnacle rising from the depths to within 20 feet (6 m) of the surface. Due to its unprotected location, the site should only be dived on calm days and with a professional dive guide. It is named after the *Santa Monica*, a 19th century wooden schooner whose belly was torn open by the submerged rock, but which managed to extricate itself, only to sink in shallow water near St. John. Some divers still comb the surge-swept shallows looking for brass spikes from the ship. But it's the marine life and topography that make this such an outstanding dive. The fact that it is not often dived also adds to its appeal, and probably keeps the more wary sea creatures from moving off.

The mooring pin is located on the flats to the south of the summit of the pinnacle. A slow

Protruding from a protective groove along the bottom of this sea star's arm are grasping tube feet. They serve both to capture prey and move the sea star at a surprisingly rapid pace over the sea floor.

circumnavigation of the rock formation will reveal many different habitats: protected crevices, current-caressed points and long rocky ridges. The top is craggy and covered with delicate fire coral. There is a fascinating round "sink hole" that drops down 25 feet (8 m) to a sandy bottom and is great fun to explore. The southern side of the pinnacle is a gorgonian and sea fan-covered wall. At the far point scan the blue water for pelagic fish— Atlantic spadefish, horse-eye jacks, mackerels and kingfish frequently swing by the point.

A school of half a dozen curious barracuda will often escort divers back towards the boat. The bottom here appears to be flat and nondescript, but as you get closer to the main pinnacle two ledge formations rise up on either side and you're funneled into a fascinating bowl. The sides are honeycombed ledges jampacked with queen angelfish, black durgons, filefishes, fairy basslets and groupers. From here divers can explore the other radiating ridges and come across even more marine life—perhaps a turtle or sleeping nurse shark. The clarity of the water, the intriguing topography, and plentiful marine life encounters make this a great dive and a photographer's dream.

8. BROWN PANTS

DEPTH:	10-40 FEET
	(3-12 M)
LEVEL:	ADVANCED
ACCESS:	BOAT
ANCHORAGE:	THE BIGHT;
	BENURES BAY

The south shore of Norman Island is compelling in its primitive beauty: rugged cliffs descend into the breaking surf, long tortured fingers of rock reach out just beneath the surface of the sea, and nowhere can the hand of man been seen. It's a world away from the yachting lifestyle found on the other side of the island. Brown Pants Point is the first point you encounter as you come around Norman Island from the east to this wild south coast.

Due to its shallow depths and exposure to

the predominate trade winds and seas, Brown Pants should only be dived on the calmest days. Otherwise, the surge thundering through the canyons and grottos can be overpowering. But the remote and exposed location and the resultant lack of divers means that this can be an action-packed site. Many years ago, when Annie and Duncan Muirhead were running *Misty Law*, the first liveaboard in the BVI, they were exploring this point as a possible dive site. Several large bull sharks rounded a corner and chased them back to their boat, and the site was named.

Descending to the mooring pin in about 40 feet (12 m) of water you'll be within sight of the point, which rises abruptly from the flat, almost barren sea floor. The water is usually clear here. When you first descend, look out into the blue for turtles and eagle rays. Then move up shallower, toward the underwater cliffs. Small gangs of curious barracuda loiter outside the rocks like demure juvenile delinquents—capable of doing damage but not really up to it. The dive consists of exploring the numerous canyons and grottos that are defined by the network of ridges extending from shore.

The open space between the ridges is paved with small rocks lying between sofa-sized boulders. Look for pairs of large whitespotted filefish peering coyly from around these boulders, trying to decide if the bubbling strangers are much of a threat. Black durgon and schools of palmetto are easily seen against the white frothy surf as they mill about in the breaking water above the ridges. Further back in the canyons, timid queen angelfish will tease you with a splash of color as they flee.

Many barracuda seem to take a perverse pleasure in following novices and making them nervous. But generally, they're over-rated villains and pose no threat to sightseeing divers and snorkelers.

BVI NATIONAL PARKS TRUST

Up until very recently there were minimal pressures threatening the natural beauty and wildlife of the British Virgin Islands. But as the pace of development accelerates, there are ever greater demands placed on a finite area with limited resources. It has become critically important to safeguard the BVI's scenic beauty, wildlife and areas of special natural and historic significance.

Most divers are aware of the BVI National Parks Trust through their dive site moorings program. This ongoing project of installing and managing environmentally-sound moorings at most of the BVI's established dive sites has become one of the Caribbean's most successful. But this is just a small part of what the NPT does.

The National Parks Trust is also responsible for managing the Territory's parks and protected areas, including marine parks. The NPT is working to protect various endangered species, such as marine turtles and the endemic Anegada Rock iguana. They are replanting Sage Mountain with native hard woods like mahogany. A critical project now being undertaken is the stabilization and preservation of the historic copper mine on Virgin Gorda. The beautiful botanic garden in Road Town is testimony to their efforts. Many other essential projects are planned and the establishment of additional protected areas is necessary. Their goal is not simply preservation but to also make these special places accessible to residents and visitors alike, and to increase everyone's understanding and appreciation of the natural BVI.

You can help preserve one of the most beautiful places on earth by becoming a Friend of the BVI National Parks Trust. Your donation will enable the Trust to continue its work. Membership entitles you to receive the Trust's newsletter and bulletin updates, and be invited on special tours.

Membership dues are $20. Please make your check out to:

Friends of the National Parks Trust
Ministry of Natural Resources
Road Town, Tortola, British Virgin Islands

There is a large open cave in one of the canyons. A dive light will reveal all the glorious brilliant colors of the encrusting sponges that grow in the shadows.

Caution. If there is any kind of swell, be very careful of the resulting surge for it is amplified as it rolls down the canyons. The cave can be dangerous then, both for the diver and the delicate marine growth. Take your time to explore every dead-end alley and little recess, for there is a wealth of life hidden here.

9. SPY GLASS (S)

DEPTH:	10-60 FEET
	(6-18 M)
LEVEL:	NOVICE
ACCESS:	BOAT
ANCHORAGE:	BENURES BAY;
	THE BIGHT

This is a friendly mini-wall on the north shore of Norman, just east of Benures Bay, that parallels the shoreline and drops steeply from 20 feet (6 m) on the top to a fine sand bottom at 60 feet (18 m). It is named after Spy Glass Hill on Norman Island where pirates once kept lookout for laden merchant ships. Start your dive swimming east (the reef on your right) along the bottom of the drop-off. If there is any current you'll be swimming into it, which will make your swim back that much easier. The wall is festooned with large sea fans and beautiful purple tube sponges. Many little fishes, such as damselfishes, wrasses, and tobaccofish can be found along the bottom of the wall and tucked into little holes in the reef. Don't forget to look out into the blue water on your left where you might catch a glimpse of an eagle ray, turtle, tarpon, spadefishes or at least a stingray foraging in the soft bottom.

Returning to the mooring along the top of the wall where there is good snorkeling, you're likely to see schools of blue tang converging on the bottom to graze on algae, as well as squid in mid-water and houndfish near the surface. In the shallows are colossal coral heads capped by magnificent sea fans. Beneath

them, lurking in the shadows are schools of small grunts. On top, amid the sea fans and huge feather dusters, are the cleaning stations established by small gobies.

Peter Island

10. CARROT SHOAL

DEPTH:	15-60 FEET
	(5-21 M)
LEVEL:	INTERMEDIATE
ACCESS:	BOAT
ANCHORAGE:	WHITE BAY;
	BENURES BAY

Carrot Shoal, off the southwest tip of Peter Island, is another open water site with all the adventure, superior visibility and big fish encounters this promises. Although Carrot Shoal is sheltered slightly by Peter Island, it still is exposed to the sea swells that roll in from the southeast and should only be dived when it's calm, as the surge effect of the waves is magnified by the shape of the shoal.

Carrot Shoal is shaped like a railroad train parked on an underwater platform. The platform rises abruptly from a 60- to 70-foot (18-21 m) bottom and levels off at 40 feet (12 m); then the shoal itself rises straight up to scratch at the surface. It's quite narrow and extends for several hundred feet. It is cut through in several places, which gives it the appearance of separate railway cars. From the mooring, swim clockwise around the formation. Spend the time to fully investigate the abundance of creatures living under the ledge on the edge of the platform: large green moray eels, tiny fairy basslets and reclusive lobsters. Toward the far end of the formation a large overhang rears up. Beneath it look for the

Like tiny denizens of Jurrasic Park, sailfin blennies live in small holes on the sea floor and dart out to grab food. When another sailfin blenny threatens its territory, it will display its sail fin and attack the intruder.

Black coral, protected by law, adorns some of the reefs around Peter Island. Its delicate fine branches are especially photogenic when backlit by the sun.

uncommon longsnout butterflyfish, as well as colorful Spanish and spotted lobsters. Past the end of the "train" there is a lovely low archway worthy of the side trip.

Returning along the other side of the shoal, there is a cut through the rock that is usually full of Spanish grunts. More undercut ledges and a small canyon provide plenty of interest all the way back to the boat. Actually, exploring the top of the ridge is a little complicated as the surge there can be quite pronounced when there is any kind of sea swell. However, beautiful orange-colored strawberry tunicates can be found tucked away in fire coral-encrusted holes and black durgons will zip into fissures in the rock to hide.

11. BLACK TIP REEF

DEPTH:	25-65 FEET
	(8-20 M)
LEVEL:	NOVICE
ACCESS:	BOAT
ANCHORAGE:	WHITE BAY;
	LITTLE HARBOUR

Black Tip Reef is located off the northwest tip of Peter Island between Rock Hole and Rogers Points, and is typical of the mini-walls that are common around Peter Island. The reef starts fairly close to shore, gently sloping down to about 25 to 35 feet (8-11 m) of water and then abruptly drops to 65 feet (20 m). Along the top, back from the drop-off, are large coral heads towering over the rest of the low relief reef. At their bases, shy brightly colored juvenile fishes will play hide-and-seek with underwater photographers. Towards the edge of the wall, small formations of staghorn, brain and star coral cover the bottom, and sea fans and gorgonians wave in the current. Squirrelfishes, trumpetfish and small groupers are common in this protective habitat.

The wall itself is adorned with black coral and spiraled wire coral. Look for banded coral shrimp and immense feather duster worms amid the sponges. There is a colony of garden eels in the sand at the bottom. Keep an eye out for turtles cruising along the drop-off.

12. *RHONE* ANCHOR

DEPTH:	40-65 FEET
	(12-20 M)
LEVEL:	INTERMEDIATE
	TO ADVANCED
ACCESS:	BOAT
ANCHORAGE:	GREAT HARBOUR

This calm-water site outside the mouth of Great Harbour on the western side of Peter Island, is where the Royal Mail Steamer *Rhone* was anchored on October 29, 1867. On that fateful day, the *Rhone* was shipwrecked on the rocks off Salt Island, four miles distant. As the fury of the hurricane increased, the crew of the

Photographers should be aware that even common subjects take on dramatic proportions when photographed from a low angle, looking up.

The magnificent feather duster worm conceals its worm-like body in a parchment-like tube. The extended "feather duster" is both gill and feeding apparatus. It is very sensitive and withdraws quickly when approached.

Rhone first jettisoned all loose items on deck. When the massive anchor chain snagged while they were trying to escape the onslaught, they abandoned over 300 feet (91 m)of chain and the *Rhone*'s main anchor. After extensive research, George Marler discovered the site in 1974.

From the mooring—the westernmost of the two outside Great Harbour—swim south over several large coral mounds sporting tree-like black coral bushes until you intersect the anchor chain. Turning right (west) will lead to the 15-foot (5 m) anchor leaning up against a coral head with one large fluke buried in the sand. The anchor and the individual links of the chain are simply massive and overgrown with delicate corals and tunicates. The chain itself runs for several hundred feet, alternately draped over the mounds or buried in the sand. There is another old anchor nearby, and a few pieces of *Rhone* china and old bottles embedded in the coral. Most of the jettisoned china was recovered years ago, long before the site achieved the protective status of a BVI National Park.

We recommend that you dive the site with an experienced local guide who can point out the various artifacts. Otherwise you could easily miss it all. The limited reef life and mediocre visibility aren't strong enough to stand on their own. To be candid, if it wasn't for the massive anchor and chain, and our fascination with the details of disaster, this site probably wouldn't be dived very often.

*Perhaps not as romantic as a sunken
ship, the cars and trucks of Truck
Reef are still a lot of fun to explore.
Combined with several huge old
anchors and large black coral trees,
the site offers an interesting 100-foot
(30 m) wall dive.*

13. TRUCK REEF

DEPTH:	35-100 FEET
	(11-30 M)
LEVEL:	INTERMEDIATE
ACCESS:	BOAT
ANCHORAGE:	GREAT HARBOUR

In the 1950's as Tortola prepared for the visit
of Queen Elizabeth, there was a "Clean for the
Queen" campaign to rid the island of unsightly
derelict cars. So they loaded up a barge and
dumped a load of cars and trucks in the sea
outside the mouth of Great Harbour. At least

that's one version of how the vehicles got to
Truck Reef. Others include ill-fated drag races
on the (too thin) ice one very cold winter when
the Sir Francis Drake Channel froze over!
Regardless, Truck Reef is still an intriguing
dive, not so much for the vehicles as for the
steep drop-off festooned with massive black
coral trees and several huge anchors.

As there is no mooring on this site, and it's
located well offshore with no obvious
landmarks, the odds of finding the exact
location on your own are pretty small. From a
boat properly positioned by a knowledgeable
dive guide, swim toward the drop-off and
you're likely to encounter at least one of the
trucks. Silly photos can be taken sitting in the
driver's seat at six fathoms below. Keep the
reef to your right as you slowly descend the

wall and look for the huge anchors embedded in the coral. They can be difficult to make out as they are completely overgrown and have no telltale chain. The black coral trees here are mammoth and protected by both BVI and US laws. Photographers seem to get their best results by shooting them from below and silhouetting the delicate branches against the surface with available light only. Large tube sponges line the top of the wall. Make sure you navigate back to your boat underwater as boats sailing by will not be on the lookout for divers on the surface.

Caution. Remember, this is one of the BVI's deeper dives, almost 100 feet (30 m), so don't dally too long at depth.

14. THE *FEARLESS & WILLIE T*

DEPTH:	30-85 FEET
	(9-26 M)
LEVEL:	INTERMEDIATE
ACCESS:	BOAT
ANCHORAGE:	GREAT HARBOUR

On the eastern side of the mouth of Great Harbour is another of the Peter Island's mini-wall dives, this one with the added attraction of two sunken ships to explore. The *Fearless* (rumored to be a sistership-of-sorts to the famous *Calypso*) was intentionally sunk in 1986. The original plans called for it to be placed at the base of the drop-off at Truck Reef, but sinking vessels often have their own plans and it ended here, about half a mile away. In the summer of 1995 the *Fearless* was joined by the *Willie T*, the very popular floating bar and restaurant formerly of Norman Island. Just out of sight and to the south of the *Fearless*, the *Willie T* sits upright on the bottom. Those divers who previously enjoyed multitudes of rum and cokes at the bar, might find the new ambiance a little disconcerting. But all-in-all it makes this site just that much more interesting.

Like Truck and Blacktip Reefs, the visibility here is usually less than outstanding and the fishes are not known for their awesome size, but the wall is covered with monster-black coral trees and the reef is endowed with a generous population of small brightly colored tropical fishes. There is also the 100-foot (30 m) *Fearless* to explore. She sits upright on the sand in 80 feet (24 m) of water, right next to the wall. Beautiful tunicates and other encrusting marine life are beginning to soften the *Fearless*'s stark lines.

Because both these ships are wood and subject to decay, it is recommended that divers do not actually penetrate the wrecks. But great fun can be had swimming around the intact wheelhouse, zooming up and down the various ladders and gangways, and even "ordering a cold one" at the *Willie T*'s old bar. A school of bar jacks hangs out on the mast of the *Fearless*, and great Truk Lagoon-like photographs of the mast and the school of fish silhouetted against a sunburst can be made here. A large jewfish has been spotted on the *Fearless* many times, but an appearance is not

The wreck of the Fearless *lies in the protected waters off Great Harbour, Peter Island. It is a good dive to do from your own boat. Just don't venture inside; instead explore the surrounding reef.*

Observant divers will notice these parasitic isopods clinging onto the faces of butterflyfishes, groupers and, in this case, a squirrelfish. Fishes don't have hands to pull them off and so are stuck with them for years. Cleaning stations offer no relief.

guaranteed. Barracuda, tangs, goatfishes and their brethren are the standard fare.

Great Harbour is almost always calm, so the *Fearless* and *Willie T* (as well as Truck Reef and the Anchor of the *Rhone*) are great fall-back dives when the seas occasionally kick up.

15. SHARK POINT

DEPTH:	25-80 FEET
	(8-24 M)
LEVEL:	ADVANCED
ACCESS:	BOAT
ANCHORAGE:	NONE

The rocky southern tip of Peter Island continues underwater as a ridge rising above a fairly nondescript bottom. The area is an undersea crossroads with schools of pelagics sweeping through, mingling with the schools of residents, and then zooming off again. Visibility can be exceptional—over 100 feet (30 m)—due to the site's location in the open ocean.

The mooring places the boat over a shallow, fire coral-blanketed saddle on the ridge. It can sometimes be a tough swim against the prevailing current from the boat up over the top of the ridge and down to the other side. There is a small cave just to your left as you come over the saddle. As you turn right and follow the ridge away from shore, a condo-sized rock abuts a matching-sized dog leg dent in the ridge. Here you can find shelter from the current and if it is particularly strong, this is a great vantage point to watch the schools of black durgon, horse-eye jacks and the occasional marauding barracuda cavorting above the current-swept craggy edge of the ridge. Continuing out along the base of the ridge there is a small tunnel that cuts through it and into a canyon formed by a second parallel ridge. Queen angelfish, whitespotted filefish, groupers and all the different species of butterflyfishes frequent this area.

Deeper, there is a series of mini-ridges. We once spotted a large jewfish and a sizable nurse shark resting on top of one another in a low archway here. This is an exciting place to scan the blue water horizon as you never know what may pass by; turtles, large jacks and even the odd shark have been sighted here. Head back to the boat, hugging the lee side of the ridge to avoid any current.

Virtually a second separate dive site is the maze-like system of alleyways and caves that pockmark the shoreline in less than 20 feet (6 m) of water. There is one cave with five separate entrances. But diving here requires flat calm conditions and advanced buoyancy skills.

Caution. This is an advanced dive because it is exposed to the prevailing swells and sometimes has strong current. Snorkeling should only be attempted in the shallows on calm days by experienced snorkelers.

Dead Chest Island

16. DEAD CHEST WEST

DEPTH:	15-55 FEET
	(5-17 M)
LEVEL:	INTERMEDIATE
ACCESS:	BOAT
ANCHORAGE:	DEAD MAN'S BAY

This is a fun knock-about dive on the west side

There are over 300 species of nudibranchs worldwide, each one more fantastic than the next. This sea goddess is just over an inch long. The name nudibranch means "naked gill" and the tuft on the animal's back are its gills.

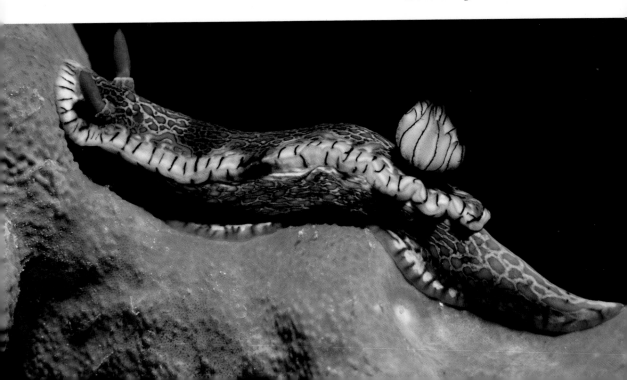

A small sharknose goby sits on a great star coral formation waiting for a client to show up at its cleaning station. A diver can sometimes be "cleaned" by slowly presenting his hand to the fish.

Even a cute little fish like the sharpnose puffer can be an aggressive predator if given the opportunity. This one has found a brittle star crawling out in the open and has bitten off an arm.

of Dead Chest Island. While a tour will guarantee you see all the highlights, Dead Chest West is a good place to follow your own nose and make your own discoveries. Just be sure you explore the shallows at the end of the dive.

Directly behind the boat, along an unobtrusive spur-and-groove formation, is a low ridge with an archway. Schools of brightly colored grunts inhabit the arch and shy mahogany snappers will drift off as you approach. Under the overhang, look for beautiful encrusting sponges, fairy basslets swimming upside down, and the antenna of small spotted lobsters. A light will help. There are several other overhangs in the vicinity. Following the next sand groove towards the shallows, you'll encounter some high rocks with lobster dens at their bases. Nearby is a spectacular mushroom-shaped coral head that sprouts up from the bottom. Redspotted hawkfish, wrasses, gobies and chromis all buzz around its top. Juvenile Spanish hogfish operate an active cleaning station here; sit back and watch the patrons come in and take their turn.

The dramatic topside cliff face continues underwater and a slow cruise along it will reveal a fascinating topography with a few surprises. There are two caves. One has a triangular opening and is filled with glassy sweepers and banded coral shrimp, as well as a few spiny urchins. The other, at the far end of a large bowl, cuts into the back of a mammoth monolith. A large, green moray eel is often resident. For divers who enjoy shallow water exploration, there is a fascinating maze of alleys, arches and ravines just past the second cave.

17. CORAL GARDENS (S)

DEPTH:	15-35 FEET
	(5-11 M)
LEVEL:	NOVICE
ACCESS:	BOAT
ANCHORAGE:	DEAD MAN'S BAY

Coral Gardens is a friendly site on the northeast side of Dead Chest Island. Local dive shops often bring resort course students here for their first dive. Swimming forward from the mooring there are scores of large coral mounds capped with beautiful and healthy formations of brain, star and sheet corals. Filefishes, chub, large snappers and barracuda patrol the mid-water realm, while goatfishes, grunts, damselfishes and squirrelfishes inhabit the reef structure along with large sea fans and beautiful gorgonians. Numerous overhangs host brightly colored encrusting sponges and jawfish live in burrows in the sand. Closer to shore there is a long overhang. Good luck trying to find the hidden anchor. Hint—it's near a flat tunnel. While most BVI dive sites consist primarily of coral-festooned rock (fascinating though that topography may be), this site is rich in massive luxuriant coral heads—a true coral garden.

You can snorkel at this site, but only on very calm days. Watch out for boat traffic.

18. PAINTED WALLS

DEPTH:	20-40 FEET
	(6-12 M)
LEVEL:	INTERMEDIATE
ACCESS:	BOAT
ANCHORAGE:	DEAD MAN'S BAY

Another of the BVI's top ten dive sites, Painted Walls is a series of technicolor box canyons located at the convoluted end of a long rocky ridge protruding from the southeast tip of Dead Chest Island. This ridge, awash with breaking waves, separates into several fingers that reach out towards the open ocean.

Directly behind the boat, when the National Parks Trust mooring is picked up, is a wonderful little reef complete with undercut ledges, large perfect brain coral heads, lots of fishes and an active cleaning station. Don't dally here at the beginning of the dive, but explore this area at the end if you still have air and film left. From the mooring swim towards the ridge and follow it out to sea. The water here is often very clear with well over 100-foot (30 m) visibility, making it easy to spot angelfishes, queen triggerfish and chub scurrying about their business. The rocks that

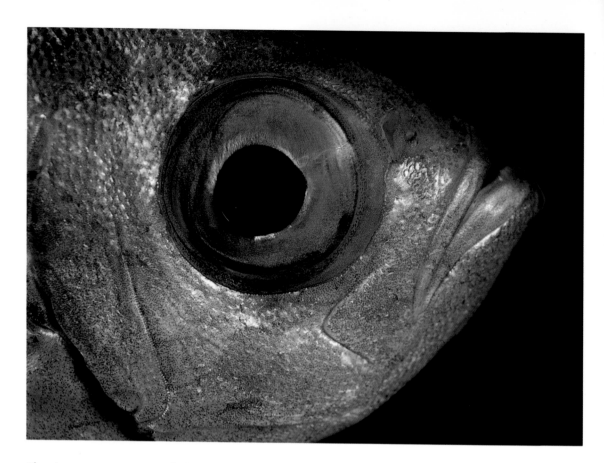

The glasseye snapper generally lurks in the shadows under overhangs. If a diver moves in slowly and quietly, it is possible to get close enough to look into the fish's deep, dark eye.

make up the ridge and its protrusions are covered with golden colored fire coral, along with gorgonians and sea fans. There is a shortcut into the first canyon which can be found by swimming over the ridge just forward of the last breaking rock. Down you'll fall into a high-walled stone dungeon with crenelated rock battlements ripping the bottoms out of the waves rolling by overhead. Exit this canyon by hugging the far side and sneaking out single file between the wall and a massive sponge-covered boulder.

Follow the contours past a beautiful pillar coral formation into the main canyon. The floor is paved with smooth, rounded rocks and the spaces between them are a micro-habitat. By gently picking up or rolling selected rocks to the side, you can enter a miniature world of tiny brittle stars, little snails and nudibranchs, delicate sponges and fragile worms. Please

leave this world secure from predators by gently returning the rocks to their original place. The floor gradually slopes up to less than 30 feet (9 m) and the walls narrow as you near the end of the 120-foot-long (36 m) canyon. Straight ahead a narrow tunnel/chimney slopes towards the surface, which, aside from the fact that it doesn't lead anywhere, should not be entered in order to prevent damaging diver or marine life. On the right is the famous sponge-encrusted tunnel that gives rise to the site's name. While all the walls of the canyons are sponge-encrusted, it is here, in the shade of the tunnel, that they reach their zenith. Bring a dive light to reveal their full technicolor glory: dayglo reds and pinks, iridescent purples and blues, stark white, fluorescent yellows and orange, and more. It is difficult to capture this singular beauty on film as the result is usually simply a

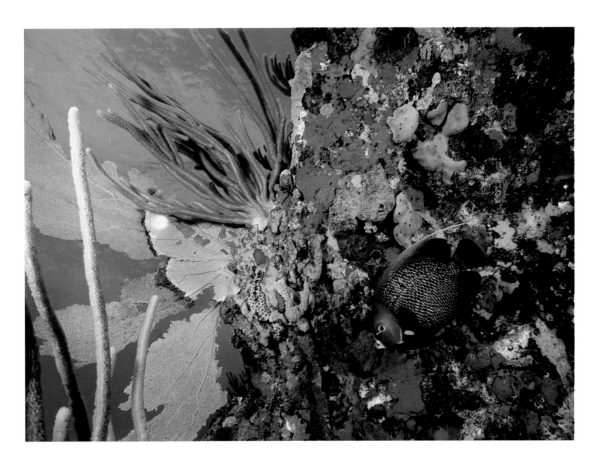

Getting low and shooting up usually creates a more powerful image. The brilliant colors that photographers seek are often hidden on the undersides of ledges and overhangs.

chaos of color. Attempts with all lens formats will have equal chance of success. The photograph on the cover of this book was taken here.

Pass through this tunnel into a very shallow "tide pool" which is brightly lit and full of fishes. Now it is time to return down the canyon and around the point to the mooring. Because you cannot swim directly from this furthest point back to the boat but must go back around the ridge tip, we recommend that you dive with a guide who will pace your tour to ensure that you have enough air to return safely underwater. A typical dive here lasts close to an hour and every minute is a treat.

Caution. Only visit Painted Walls on calm days. When it is rough, the surge rolling through the canyons turns the site into a washing machine with an extra spin cycle.

Between Salt and Dead Chest

19. BLONDE ROCK

DEPTH:	10-65 FEET
	(3-18 M)
LEVEL:	ADVANCED
ACCESS:	BOAT
ANCHORAGE:	NONE

This is one of the authors' favorite dives. Located between Dead Chest and Salt Islands, it offers good visibility, lots of big fishes, fascinating topography, a taste of adventure, and photo opportunities galore. Blonde Rock is a set of two pinnacles, out in the middle of nowhere, that rise from 60 feet (18 m) to within 15 feet (5 m) of the surface. Occasionally current-swept and the only topographic feature of any significance in the Salt Island Passage, Blonde Rock is a natural magnet attracting all kinds of marine life—turtles, schools of jacks, cobia, barracuda and even the occasional shark. The twin fire coral-encrusted peaks (hence the "blonde" designation) rise from a gorgonian-covered plateau at 35 to 40 feet (11-12 m). All the way around this sheer-walled plateau is an amazing system of undercuts, ledges, canyons, tunnels and companion rocks.

There are two NPT moorings on the site and both are nicely situated. Descend from your boat and regroup on the plateau before dropping to the sandy bottom at 60 feet (18 m). Below the western mooring, a vertical fissure slices through the edge of the plateau. A series of separated formations nearby are worthy of exploration. Undercuts, narrow passages and little caverns predominate. One such hollow is filled with blackbar soldierfish.

Following the formation to the east, a large ledge breaks the wall into a two-tier climb. While many divers cruise along the outside edge, make sure you ascend slightly to explore this fish-covered flat and the honeycombed ledge behind it. This is a very active area with schools of chub, horse-eye and bar jacks, and creole wrasse as well as tomtates, coneys and parrotfishes. Just past this ledge Blonde Rock is carved out to form a spectacular amphitheater —a large steep-walled bowl that never fails to impress divers. The severely undercut walls hide a shadowy world filled with glasseye snapper, graysby and large crabs. With a flashlight, the brilliant colors of the sponges, coralline algae and cup coral will leap out at you. The craggy upper lip of the wall is adorned with sea fans, deep-water gorgonians and a strange green-stalked colonial hydroid. After fully exploring the extensive undercut and the bowl itself, with its school of brilliant yellow French grunts, climb out of the back of the bowl and stop at the pit right at the edge. A small cave in the back of the pit hosts a perpetually spiraling school of glassy sweepers.

If you're diving without a local guide or are low on air, head back across the plateau to the mooring, looking out for angelfishes, triggerfishes and pelagics en route. But if you have plenty of air left and your guide is game,

cut across the plateau through the notch between the pinnacles and explore the south side. If the current is running, there is generally a lot of action here. While you won't find an extensive ledge system, there are a couple of massive ridges protruding from the western peak. There's a shortcut tunnel through the base of one ridge into the next canyon. Keeping the rock to your right, work your way back around to the mooring.

Before the NPT moorings were installed, you could not even find Blonde Rock without a

While we usually encourage slow-paced diving with frequent stops for a closer look, every so often it's nice to gently cruise along without stopping, taking in the overall ambiance of the coral reef.

local dive guide. But now, because it's relatively easy to locate the mooring balls, some bareboaters are setting off to explore the site without professional supervision, adequate experience or local knowledge. We strongly recommend that this dive be made with a local dive guide and only when the seas are calm. Blonde Rock is completely exposed to the prevailing weather, subject to strong current and a long way from land. Navigation here can be complicated as the site is disorienting. You'll get much more out of the experience with someone to show you the highlights and guide you back to the boat.

Caution. If you insist on doing it on your own, dive only when seas are calm and check for current; it can be very strong. If it is too strong, don't make the dive. If the current is moderate-to-strong or picks up after you enter, limit your dive to exploring the lee side of the rock and that way you won't have to fight the current. Plan your dive so that you will return to the mooring slightly upcurrent and get a free ride as part of your final ascent. Avoid surfacing away from the boat.

Salt Island

(*See next chapter for RMS* RHONE *site 20.*)

21. *RHONE* REEF (S)

DEPTH:	10-50 FEET
	(3-15 M)
LEVEL:	ADVANCED
ACCESS:	BOAT
ANCHORAGE:	LEE BAY;
	SETTLEMENT BAY

turtles, occasional shark

Just around the corner from the wreck of the *Rhone* is a marvelous site aptly named *Rhone* Reef. It is possible to dive the reef (or at least part of it) from the moorings on the *Rhone*. In fact, dive guides often take divers who have repeatedly dived the wreck over to Rhone Reef, while others in the group explore the stern section of the wreck. However, to fully

The salt ponds on Salt Island are still worked. Sea water is allowed to flood the ponds. As the water evaporates in the hot sun, a salty crust is left along the pond's edge.

A diver pauses at the entrance of a U-shaped tunnel which is typical of the convoluted reef structure that makes up Rhone Reef.

experience the glory of *Rhone* Reef we recommend that you use the mooring installed specifically on the site.

Like many BVI sites, *Rhone* Reef has both deep and shallow components, each equally fascinating to explore. In 50 feet (15 m) of water, just shoreward of the mooring line is a vaguely defined pit with spectacular overhangs and meandering branches. The encrusting sponges beneath the overhangs are as brightly colored as any. Many fishes, such as graysbys, squirrelfishes and big porgies loiter in these protective recesses. Upward angle photographs, with strobe light illuminating the sponges and the brighter surface as a background, are easily gotten here as there is plenty of working space. Following the contours toward land there is a magnificent dual formation of brain and pillar coral that also serves as a cleaning station.

Leaving the lush coral seascapes behind, there is an area of smooth round rocks before you reach the actual shoreline cliff with waves breaking above. It's quite shallow here, 20 feet (6 m) and less, so be careful of surge and wave action. Swimming into the bowl on your left, there will be dramatic surf overhead, and two caves and a tunnel straight ahead. Turtles and, occasionally, tarpon are spotted here. The two caves are beautiful to look into, but please resist the temptation to venture inside as the walls are covered with fragile marine life. One cave is filled with a swirling mass of glassy sweepers and the further recesses of the other are lit by a rooftop skylight. To the left is a U-shaped tunnel that, in addition to being a place of singular beauty, will also lead out of the bowl. Continuing along the shallows on the other side will lead back to the *Rhone*, or curving back to your left (swim in mid-water to avoid going deeper at the end of your dive) will bring you back to the mooring.

Snorkeling. Snorkeling should only be attempted on calm days by experienced snorkelers.

Viewing breaking surf on Rhone
*Reef from underwater can be
exciting; just don't get too close.*

Between Cooper and Salt

22. VANISHING ROCKS

DEPTH:	15-45 FEET
	(5-14 M)
LEVEL:	INTERMEDIATE
ACCESS:	BOAT
ANCHORAGE:	SETTLEMENT BAY
	MANCHIONEEL
	BAY

A popular dive, Vanishing Rocks is a very healthy shallow reef due to the currents that sweep through the passage between Cooper and Salt Islands. These currents, which when strong can make the site undivable, nurture its many species of corals and support a large population of reef fishes.

Locating the site is easy enough. Just follow the ridge line of Cistern Point on Cooper Island a third of the way across to Salt Island. There are two mooring buoys located adjacent to the barely breaking pinnacle peak. The near mooring is a little too close to the rock for a large boat or even a smaller one left unattended. Be especially careful of wind shifts or an outgoing current pushing the boat back against the rock.

The underwater ridge extends off to either side of the breaking pinnacle and is surrounded by lesser formations pockmarked with overhangs, ledges and undercuts. Due to the shallow depths it is usually possible to circumnavigate the site in a single dive. If a strong current is flowing, however, it would be prudent to do a very detailed exploration of the protected side only. Descending from the boat will place you on a slope covered with gorgonians and small barrel sponges. Closer to the pinnacle there is a sandy area, surrounded by rocks and ledges. This is a great place to lie down on your belly, get your face in close and leisurely observe the inhabitants such as anemones and shrimp, jawfishes, and blennies. Staying in the sand collar you can start your circumnavigation, either to the left or right. Heading left (with the rock on your right)

Glassy sweepers lurk in caves by day, venturing out to feed at night. Their gentle swaying in the surge can be mesmerizing.

The current-bathed reefs of Vanishing Rock are particularly colorful. Though currents can complicate diving, they often make for more abundant marine life.

follow the contours into a small depression ringed by even more ledges and undercuts. Thick delicate coral growth, lobsters, and occasional sleeping nurse sharks can be found here. The current sweeps over this area and sheltered behind the rocks is a wealth of life.

Continuing around, winding along the sandy floor, you'll eventually reach the more exposed far side of the formation. There are two small box-canyonettes here. If conditions permit, a look at the base of the breaking rock might prove interesting. Otherwise, proceed along the deeper water a little further out and you'll reach Sergeant Major City, a large multi-spired formation of pillar coral that is positively overflowing with fish life. Sergeant majors of course, but also squirrelfishes, grunts and bigeye snappers reside here. A little further along is an outlying pillar coral formation called, you guessed it, Sergeant Major Suburbs. From here you'll have to cross over the ridge to return back to the other side. Hugging the edge of the rock will bring you to a series of overhangs where a large green moray eel is often spotted.

Caution. If the current is running hard, please err on the side of caution.

Cooper Island

23. CISTERN POINT (S)

DEPTH:	10-40 FEET
	(3-12 M)
LEVEL:	NOVICE
ACCESS:	BOAT
ANCHORAGE:	MANCHIONEEL
	BAY

On the southern end of postcard-perfect Manchioneel Bay, a rocky point carpeted with life projects out to sea. Cistern Point is a fabulous shallow dive as well as one of the better snorkeling spots. Divers from yachts anchored in front of the Cooper Island Beach Club can easily dinghy over to the dinghy mooring on the site. Tanks and refills can be arranged through the Underwater Safaris boutique and air-fill station at the Club. Commercial boats often dive here because of the sheltered conditions and quantity of fish

Little Carval Rock is a nesting site for terns. The reef and rocks surrounding the point are a very popular snorkel and dive site, especially for yachts anchored at nearby Manchioneel Bay.

life. It is also possible to dive this site from shore, but if you're on Cooper Island already you probably have access to at least a dinghy. So use it and avoid the long walk over private property carting heavy dive gear.

From either the dinghy or dive boat mooring swim up to the point and, keeping it on your left, swim leisurely around to the other side looking for the plentiful queen angelfish, thick schools of sergeant majors and chromis, as well as jacks and a traveling band of gray snappers. There is a series of shallow craters on the far side that are interesting to explore.

It is possible to cut back across the shallows at the tip of the point. However, it is not advisable to swim across the very shallow water between prominent Cistern Rock and shore. On top of the ridge there are schools of blue tang, goatfishes, beautiful anemones and active cleaning stations. Cistern Point is a great site to explore on your own or with a knowledgeable guide who can point out all the intricacies of the coral reef habitat.

24. THE *MARIE L & PAT*

DEPTH:	45-90 FEET
	(14-26 M)
LEVEL:	INTERMEDIATE
ACCESS:	BOAT
ANCHORAGE:	MANCHIONEEL
	BAY

South of Cistern Point and the Cooper Island Beach Club on Manchioneel Bay, past the first mooring at Blue Chromis Reef but before you reach Thumb Rock (Red Bluff), you'll come across a NPT mooring that marks the *Marie L*'s final resting place. The *Marie L*, a cargo boat owned by a local family, was intentionally sunk in the early 1990's to add an extra dimension of interest to a calm-water dive site. All 75 feet (23 m) of her sits in the sand in about 85 feet (26 m) of water just off a coral mini-wall. She has recently been joined by two additional wrecks: the Barge & Grill and the *Pat*, a 70-foot (21 m) tugboat.

From the mooring pin atop the reef, swim out to the edge of the wall (which roughly parallels the shore) and drop down to the bottom. Depending on the visibility, you should be able to make out the vague shape of a shipwreck looming out of the gloom about 70 feet (21 m) out from the wall. The *Pat* and the *Marie L* sit right next to each other, bow-to-stern, with a narrow gap between them. In fact the *Pat* hit and slid off the *Marie L* on her way to the bottom in early 1995. A tour around the ships is fascinating. They sit upright, leaning away from one another, with the *Pat* closer to shore. The intact hulls are a little spooky, parked as they are, upright in the sand. Be careful about venturing too far inside as this is an overhead environment, though the wheelhouses should be safe. A young jewfish has been seen around the wrecks, but is very shy and usually departs as soon as divers approach. Look under the stern of the *Marie L* for jackknife fish and spotted drums, and up on deck for grunts.

A little to the north is a nondescript wreck called the Barge & Grill. If you're the type that can't stop cruising, (or if you've done this site before) then by all means check it out, otherwise the *Marie L* and the *Pat* will probably take up most of your deep-water bottom time. There is a large colony of garden eels out in the sand. If you approach them quietly and try to control your noisy exhalation bubbles, you might be able to creep up close enough to see their beady little eyes. Otherwise, they'll tease you by retreating back into their holes just as you get within range. Stingrays can also be spotted in the sand and eagle rays are often seen soaring overhead.

Don't dally too long at this depth, but instead head back to the reef top and explore the coral ridges on the way back to the mooring. Photographers can work in the sand gullies and get low and close to their subjects without damaging the living coral.

Caution. Because the site is so convenient to the Cooper Island Beach Club and generally very calm, the *Marie L* is attractive to inexperienced divers venturing out without a local guide. Care must be taken, however, as the wreck is quite deep (80+ feet) and the reef top isn't much shallower, so air consumption can be faster than expected, and it is also possible to get into decompression complications (especially as a repetitive dive). Visit the wrecks first and then finish the dive up on the reef top beneath the mooring with plenty of air left. As always, do a 5-minute safety stop at 15 feet (5 m).

25. THUMB ROCK

DEPTH:	20-60 FEET
	(6-18 M)
LEVEL:	INTERMEDIATE
ACCESS:	BOAT
ANCHORAGE:	MANCHIONEEL
	BAY

Thumb Rock is named for the large rock that stands out from Red Bluff Point, jutting from the water like a giant thumb, and the corresponding "thumb" that rises from the sea floor to just below the surface. The mooring sits back a bit from the point and the dive consists of a slow meander along the bottom towards the point. There are ledges that undercut the shoreline as it drops away from the surface, and coral-encrusted boulders and patch reefs separated by sand areas. Large whitespotted filefish and parrotfishes cruise this area. Scrawled filefish can be found nibbling on the delicate tips of fire coral. Shy queen angelfish and more brazen French angelfish swim about in pairs, sometimes in trios.

The underwater "thumb" is quite an impressive monolith, rising sheer from the sea bed. It's covered with deep-water gorgonians, sponges, fire coral and small patches of hard corals. Fuzzy gorgonians reach out from the thumb and other boulders. Up in the shallows is a jumble of boulders. As usual, lots of fishes

Lying in the sand in 80 feet (24 m) of water, the wrecks of the Marie L *(left) and the* Pat *(right) were sunk intentionally in the lee of Cooper Island. These wrecks attract small schools of fish including goatfishes and grunts.*

hide in the concavities that form between the rounded boulders. During the late spring and early summer months, schools of tiny silvery fry congregate in the shallows and massive shiny tarpon cut through the schools, grabbing mouthfuls of the little fish.

26. MARKOE POINT

DEPTH:	30-60 FEET (9-18 M)
LEVEL:	ADVANCED
ACCESS:	BOAT
ANCHORAGE:	MANCHIONEEL BAY

Normally an aggressive predator, this Nassau grouper is eager to be cleaned. The shrimp and gobies fearlessly scamper all over its body and into its mouth and gills, removing dead skin, scales and small ectoparasites.

Markoe Point lies on the lonely southeastern tip of Cooper Island, jutting out into the open Caribbean. When you round this back side of Cooper, all the hustle and bustle of the BVI falls behind and you could be diving the most isolated point on earth—except for the perfectly positioned NPT mooring buoy.

The mooring sits behind the point, enjoying a little protection from prevailing trade winds. Forward of the mooring is a delightful gully that runs along the point, with a sheer cliff on one side and an exquisitely undercut coral ridge on the other. Look for lobsters deep in the crevices, and schools of black durgon and snapper out in the open. Swim around the point and cruise along the base of the cliff. It bottoms out abruptly on a sand and rock-strewn plain. Looking up the precipitous rock face you'll see thick clouds of swirling white foam as the waves break against the cliff. With

a little imagination it might even appear to be the mists of time obscuring the heights of Mt. Olympus. Honestly though, it's not that deep a dive. Be careful about going too shallow as you don't want to be caught up in the pounding waves.

Along the bottom of the cliff, big solitary snappers and groupers patrol. A good turn-around point is the tall fissure that cleaves vertically through the wall. Inside lots of smaller grunts, snappers and blackbar soldierfish hide from predators. On the way back there is a shallow saddle that cuts through the tip of the point. If it's too rough, go the long way, otherwise use the surge to shoot through the gap. Spend your remaining air exploring the gully and the shallows.

Between Cooper and Ginger

27. CARVAL ROCK

DEPTH:	15-90 FEET
	(5-27 M)
LEVEL:	ADVANCED
ACCESS:	BOAT
ANCHORAGE:	MANCHIONEEL
	BAY

Sitting outside the gap between Cooper and Ginger Islands, Carval Rock looks a little like a Caravel sailing ship of days past. At least that's supposed to be the origin of the name. This is a dive site off the beaten path, and not too many people get out here. It is a long run from the shops, exposed to both the north swell and southeast trades, and not the best-all-time dive. Nonetheless, when conditions permit and you're looking for somewhere new and different to go, try heading out to Carval.

The NPT mooring is located about halfway down the Cooper Island side of Carval. It is moderately interesting under the boat. Look for green morays and lobsters along the ledges that fall away from the rock. Closer to Carval is a jumble of huge boulders. Schools of fishes loiter in the shadows. Large whitespotted filefish, groupers, queen triggerfish and durgon move about the openings to the recesses

between the boulders. Lots of fire coral and attendant jewelfish, redlip gobies and damselfishes cover the tops of the boulders. Barracudas and occasional mackerels and kingfish are in mid-water .

There is a temptation to swim all around Carval. It is possible, but it requires that you be a strong swimmer, good on air and don't stop much to look on your way. If you just want to go a little bit and then come back, we recommend heading around the north end and exploring the shallow water around Carval and the breaking rock offshore. Sponge-covered boulders, schools of French grunts and blue tang, as well as large trumpetfish hiding in the waving gorgonians, are to be found. Spotted drums and highhats lurk in the shadows beneath the boulders.

28. DRY ROCKS EAST

DEPTH:	25-85 FEET
	(8-27 M)
LEVEL:	ADVANCED
ACCESS:	BOAT
ANCHORAGE:	MANCHIONEEL
	BAY

A barely breaking ridge just east of Cooper Island, Dry Rocks East juts out into the channel between Cooper and Ginger Islands, and acts as a natural focal point for piscine activity. It is an open water site with generally good visibility and the promise of large pelagic fish. The trade off is rougher conditions and occasionally strong currents. Nonetheless, this can be an outstanding dive. Looking out into deep blue water with your back to the ridge, watching schools of large jacks or permit sweep by, you'll know that you're at a major underwater crossroads. While it is possible to completely circumnavigate the formation in one dive, we recommend that if your bottom time and air permit, you spend a lot of time at the eastern tip where most of the action is.

At the bottom of the mooring line there is a car-sized boulder and under it a large collection of highhats (similar to spotted drums, but without the spots). Navigate from this rock in order to find the mooring when the dive is over. Swim to the ridge and proceed clockwise with the rock on your right. Looking up the craggy rock face to the breaking surf on the surface you'll spot barracuda, schools of jacks, whitespotted filefish, pufferfishes and black durgons. In the scattered rock debris on the bottom, look for various small groupers such as hinds and coneys, and parrotfishes and trunkfishes. Toward the tip of the ridge the current can be strong, so stay close to the bottom to minimize its effect. There are a few huge boulders scattered around as if they rolled down off the ridge. Under the first one, in addition to beautiful encrusting sponges and fans, a mixed school of goatfishes and grunts resides. We once encountered a turtle resting on the bottom here. It was so trusting that each diver got a chance to pet it and tickle it under the chin without the turtle being restrained in any way! The sea floor slopes down away from the ridge and if you follow the schools of Atlantic spadefish or the big French angelfish, you'll be in 80-90 feet (24-27 m) of water before you know it.

At this point, if you've sucked up too much air, you should head back to the boat the way you came. Otherwise continue on, following the far side of the ridge, towards shore. Queen triggerfish, a school of shy snappers, more angelfishes and a varied collection of reef fishes will meet you as you get shallower. There is a shortcut back to the boat over a saddle in the ridge but be especially aware of your buoyancy because of the fire coral, surge and a funneling effect of the current.

Ginger Island

29. ALICE IN WONDERLAND

DEPTH:	40-80 FEET (12-24 M)
LEVEL:	INTERMEDIATE
ACCESS:	BOAT
ANCHORAGE:	MANCHIONEEL BAY

Nestled against the cliffs on the south side of the western arm of uninhabited Ginger Island

is a very luxuriant coral reef. Called Alice in Wonderland after the huge mushroom-shaped coral heads that comprise part of this very dramatic spur-and-groove formation, this site boasts some of the largest and healthiest corals in the BVI.

Caution. Because of its exposure to the prevailing weather, this site should only be dived when conditions permit.

The upside of this lack of protection is that the water here is usually clearer than other more sheltered sites nearby. The best way to appreciate the grandeur of the coral ridges is to swim in the gullies that separate them. From this lower perspective you can look up at their height and majesty. Take the time to explore the undercuts and crevices that pockmark the corals, looking for anemones, crinoids, and little blennies and gobies. The reef top is capped with giant sea fans and gorgonian soft corals. Eagle rays, occasional sharks and shy schoolmaster snappers are seen here. Overall, it's the beauty of the corals and not the abundance of big fishes that makes this such a popular dive. Up in the shallows, between the shoreline and the coral ridges, is a sandy area where hundreds of yellowhead jawfish can be observed dancing about on their tails, just above their holes in the sand. If disturbed they zip back in, tail first. Approach slowly and you may be treated to the sight of a male incubating eggs in its mouth.

Caution. Be careful of depth. Because of the gradual slope of the bottom, it is easy to spend a lot of time on the deeper end of the site, and use up air and build up bottom time faster than planned.

30. GINGER STEPS

DEPTH:	35-100 FEET (11-30 M)
LEVEL:	INTERMEDIATE
ACCESS:	BOAT
ANCHORAGE:	MANCHIONEEL BAY

Tucked further into South Bay than Alice in Wonderland, Ginger Steps is composed of a

The common squirrelfish is often one of the first fish that new divers learn to identify.

series of huge ledges cascading down from the shallows to 100 feet (30 m). The visibility here is normally very good.

Beautiful tube sponges and sea fans grace the leading edges of the tops of the ledges. Below, look for squirrelfishes, small grunts and damselfishes. The sand between the drop-offs is so brilliantly white that the whole site seems to glow.

Down deeper, schools of pale snapper and grunts congregate in the hollows between the corals. Barracudas and juvenile angelfishes loiter around the tiny coral heads scattered in the sand beneath the mooring. As with Alice in Wonderland, Ginger Steps is best visited when seas out of the south are reasonably calm.

Tortola

31. BREWERS BAY PINNACLES

DEPTH:	25-110 FEET (8-33 M)
LEVEL:	ADVANCED
ACCESS:	BOAT
ANCHORAGE:	BREWERS BAY (IF CALM); CANE GARDEN; SOPER'S HOLE

An enjoyable dive when there's no north swell, Brewers Bay Pinnacles is located just off the western tip of the bay. It's too far from the beach to be dived as a shore dive.

Furthermore, the currents sweeping by the point and the big swells in winter make that a truly dangerous proposition. Every five or so years, someone drowns while swimming off a north side beach due to currents or waves.

Anyway, this is a safe enough dive when done from a boat, especially when accompanied by a professional dive guide. The NPT mooring is located just inside the point. From there, swim out past the point, looking out to sea for the nearest of the half dozen pinnacles. The massive pinnacles are of varying height and bulk. They rise steeply from the ocean floor, which can get as deep as 100 or more feet (30+ m). Some of them come within 30 feet (9 m) of the surface. The gaps between the sheer granite structures comprise a confusing maze of alleyways, dead ends and narrow passages. The rocks are covered with deep-water gorgonians, sea fans and fire coral. Large jacks, eagle rays and turtles are often spotted by the observant diver. Amid the rocks and reef look for lobsters, skittish queen angelfish and whitespotted filefish. The visibility here is usually only fair, 30 to 40 feet (9-12 m), due to all the nutrients in the water.

Caution. If you spend a lot of time at the deeper outskirts of the site, keep close track of your air and bottom time. And be careful of the surge and currents.

CHAPTER **IV**   THE RMS *RHONE*

HISTORY

The RMS *Rhone* is a special place, dear to the hearts of most of the dive guides who have had the privilege of extended exploration. In fact, many of the local instructors try to outdo each other in the intricacy (and occasionally the length) of their "let me tell you a bit about the wreck we're going to dive" stories. The basic meat-and-potatoes version goes something like this:

In 1865, during the height of the Industrial Revolution, the Royal Mail Steam Packet Company launched their most modern ship yet, the RMS *Rhone*. She was an all iron construction, with a length of 310 feet (94 m) and a beam of 40 feet (12 m). Sleek and fast, the *Rhone* was powered by a huge steam engine which drove one of those new-fangled propellers (earlier steamships were paddle wheel driven). She also carried two massive masts and a full complement of sails, in case that steam stuff failed to do the job.

The *Rhone* was part of a network of trans-Atlantic steamers and inter-island schooners that transported mail, passengers and cargo between England, and the West Indies and South America. The normal transfer and re-coaling station was in St. Thomas, but in the 1860's there was an outbreak of yellow fever there and the RMS Packet Company moved the station to Great Harbour, Peter Island in the British Virgin Islands.

On that fateful day, October 29, 1867, the *Rhone* was anchored at the mouth of Great Harbour along with the *Conway*, a paddle wheel driven inter-island steamer. It started as a fine clear day, but by mid-morning the weather began to deteriorate. Captain Wooley of the *Rhone* and Captain Hammock of the *Conway* conferred and concluded that, as hurricane season was supposedly over, it must be an early winter storm brewing. When the

first blast of wind and rain came howling out of the north from over Tortola, it confirmed their mistaken belief that it was a "northerly". When a lull in the storm (really the eye of a ferocious hurricane) arrived, the captains decided to weigh anchor and head for what they thought would be the sheltered anchorage of Road Harbour. Legend has it that many of the passengers from the *Conway* were transferred to the supposedly more seaworthy *Rhone* before the second onslaught of the hurricane.

The *Rhone*'s anchor snagged—probably on a coral head 60 feet (18 m) below—and her escape was delayed. Captain Wooley was forced to abandon 300 feet (91 m) of chain and his huge 3,000-pound (1,364 kg) anchor. Without her main anchor, the *Rhone* headed out to open water, looking for sea-room to ride out the storm. Swinging wide of Dead Chest Island and the submerged hazard of Blonde Rock, Wooley ventured out through the Salt Island Passage. As the eye of the hurricane passed, the second and stronger half of the hurricane swept down on the ships, this time from out of the south. The *Conway* was blown up on shore in Road Harbour. Though severely damaged she was later repaired and sailed on into obscurity. The *Rhone*, on the other hand was not so fortunate. Even with her steam engine at full speed she was no match for the

The top of the stern section of the Rhone *is within easy snorkeling distance of the surface. This school of small mouth grunts has lived in the same hollow for years. In the background, the top of the rudder post can be seen. When divers swim under this part of the wreck their exhaust bubbles roar out of the post like a smoking chimney.*

storm. The ferocious winds and towering waves drove her back against the rocks on the western tip of Salt Island.

The vicious knife edge of Black Rock Point cut through the iron hull of the ship, allowing the ocean to pour in. When the relatively cool Caribbean sea water reached the superheated boilers, there was a massive explosion. The ship was torn in two, the bow section pinwheeling away from the rocks and the stern settling where it was. Virtually all hands were lost. There were less than two dozen survivors, mostly crew.

For their heroism in rescuing the few survivors, the inhabitants of Salt Island were granted possession in-perpetuity of their tiny island. The Queen of England receives an annual payment of one bag of salt harvested from their shallow salt ponds.

The *Rhone*'s cargo was salvaged within five years of her sinking by a trio of Irish brothers using hard hat diving equipment. More recently, but prior to National Park status, a large collection of china dinner plates was recovered from Great Harbour, Peter Island, where the *Rhone* was anchored. The stern section was blown open by a US Navy underwater demolition team in the 1950's.

The great irony is that if the *Rhone* had stayed where she was in Great Harbour, she would probably have survived the hurricane, as the high hills of Peter Island would have protected her from the southerly winds of the second half of the storm.

THE DIVE

20. RMS *RHONE* (S)

DEPTH:	25-90 FEET
	(8-27 M)
LEVEL:	INTERMEDIATE;
	NOVICE WITH
	GUIDE
ACCESS:	BOAT
ANCHORAGE:	LEE BAY;
	SETTLEMENT BAY

After more than 2,000 dives on the *Rhone*, we still find it fascinating. There is hardly a better dive anywhere for either a once-in-a-lifetime tour or extensive exploration. The wreck is the perfect background for diver and fish portraits, as well as an incredible photographic subject itself. After all, it was the set for the movie *The Deep*. The fish are incredibly friendly and cooperative—they are literally scene stealers. The *Rhone* sank on the calm side of Salt Island, consequently it's almost always divable. It's deep enough to be interesting, but not so deep as to be dangerous. The stern section is scattered about, but the bow section remains intact enough for penetration. It's ideal for a two-dive tour.

The *Rhone* was one of the earliest iron ships. If it was any older, it would have been made of wood and long since rotted away. Any more recent, it would not have the unique design of a steam-sailor. She is absolutely beautiful and her sleek sailing lines still are recognizable.

Your first dive should be on the fairly intact bow section, lying on its side at 60 to 75 feet (18-23 m). You can penetrate the bow, but you'd have to try hard to get lost inside. The stern section is best dived on the second dive because you can move progressively shallower during the dive and finish in less than 30 feet (9 m) of water. While the *Rhone* can be dived on your own, we recommend that you make use of a local dive guide in order to get the most out of the dives with the least amount of hassle.

The Bow Section. With the advent of moorings strategically placed over the bow section, this has become a fairly easy dive. The only complications are depth and occasionally very strong currents. As a general precaution against the mid-water current we recommend that you descend down either the mooring line or your own weighted descent/ascent line, and in this way the current won't sweep you away from the site before you reach bottom. Avoid diving the bow from a distance. Have your boat or dinghy moored directly overhead.

A leisurely tour of the bow section will consume your allotted bottom time. As you descend, the long sweep of the wreck will materialize out of the gloom. The hull is about 150 feet (45 m) long, fairly intact and lying on its starboard side, so what were once horizontal decks are now vertical walls. Virtually all of the wooden decking has long since rotted away leaving the very dramatic

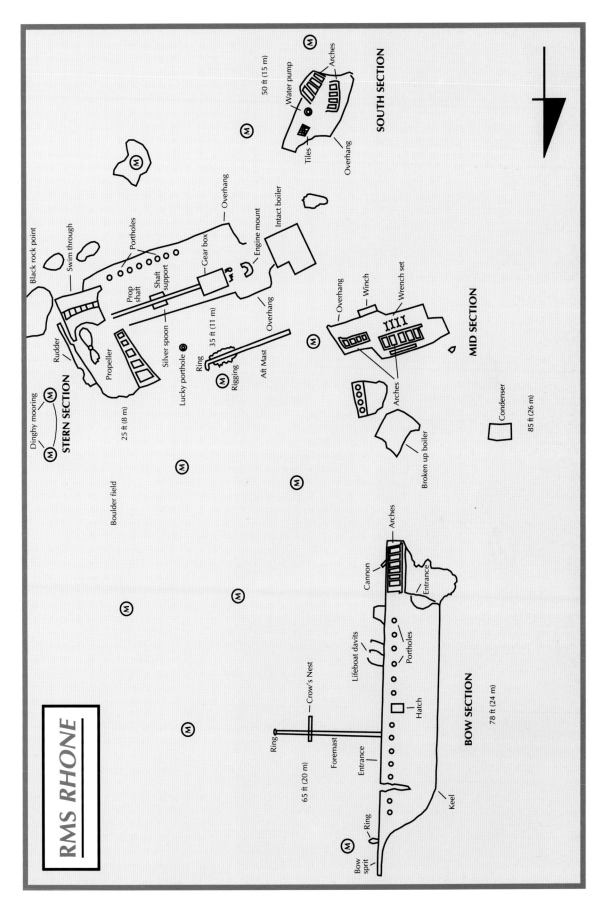

RMS *RHONE*

STERN SECTION

Black rock point
Swim through
Portholes
Overhang
Gear box
Engine mount
Intact boiler
Prop shaft
Shaft support
Silver spoon
Propeller
Rudder
Dinghy mooring
Lucky porthole
Ring
Rigging
Aft Mast
Overhang
25 ft (8 m)
35 ft (11 m)
Boulder field

SOUTH SECTION

Arches
Water pump
Tiles
Overhang
50 ft (15 m)

MID SECTION

Overhang
Winch
Wrench set
Arches
Broken up boiler
Condenser
85 ft (26 m)

BOW SECTION

Arches
Cannon
Entrance
Lifeboat davits
Portholes
Crow's Nest
Hatch
Ring
Foremast
Entrance
Keel
Bow sprit
Ring
65 ft (20 m)
78 ft (24 m)

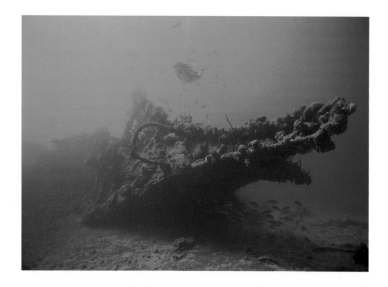

The bow section lies on its starboard side in 65 to 75 feet (20-23 m) of water. The fairly intact bow sprit, complete with the iron hoop that used to contain a huge wooden pole to which the foresails were attached, attests to the Rhone's status as an iron-hulled steam-sailor, powered by both wind and propeller.

The mid section boasts the wrench set, a winch, a beautifully encrusted overhang that used to be the outside of the hull, and two sets of arches.

The Rhone's propeller is so massive that many divers swim over it without ever seeing it. Snorkelers on the surface can make it out clearly.

This hatch, in the bow section, played an important role in the movie The Deep. *The divers entered and exited their fictional treasure ship through it.*

support beams—the famous "Greek columns." Sixty-five feet (20 m) of foremast projects out of the middle of the wreck, lying parallel to the ground. It's capped with a beautifully encrusted crow's nest. Because the mast is such an obvious landmark, it's a good idea to use it to orient yourself. Stop to make a mental note of the direction from which you approached the mast. This will help you at the end of the dive when it's time to find your way back to your boat.

You can enter the wreck just forward of the mast and then make a hard left. The interior of the wreck is fairly wide open with lots of light streaming in from various openings, including the enormous gaping hole where she was torn in half. It would be difficult to get lost inside as there are virtually no walls or corridors, but common sense and prudence suggest not trying to ferret your way into the furthest

reaches of the interior. A dive light is a definite asset, revealing brilliant colors and hidden creatures. Meandering between the beams and through shafts of light, a school of silvery tomtates makes the wreck come alive. Take the time to appreciate the exquisite orange cup coral lining the inside, as well as the mirrored ceiling created by a captured air pocket.

Exit out through the cavernous midships break. Now is a good time to check your air. If you have plenty remaining, you may want to make a hard right and swim along the ship's keel (where Jacqueline Bisset first encountered the giant moray in the movie *The Deep*). Continuing along the keel—the deepest part of the dive at 75 feet (23 m)—you'll come around to the other side by passing beneath the long pointed bowsprit. Otherwise, turn left after exiting the interior and pass by a set of columns completely covered in technicolor

BE KIND TO THE *RHONE*

The *Rhone* is the most popular dive in the BVI. In high season hundreds of divers may visit her in a single day. Seeing the need to preserve her, she was declared the territory's first Marine National Park. As such, it is illegal to remove anything (other than contemporary litter) from the wreck site. No fishing of any kind is permitted. Underwater, be gentle and try to avoid hitting or even touching the encrusting corals and sponges. Be especially careful when trying to swim through openings; when in doubt, go around. Many of the fishes and even a turtle or two are acclimatized to divers. Please don't violate their trust by grabbing them.

With the installation of moorings, anchoring is forbidden. The yellow moorings are reserved for commercial dive boats. The dinghy mooring is great for snorkelers and for diving the stern section. You should vacate your mooring as soon as you are done diving so that others can use it. As mentioned before, be careful of surface swimming because of all the boat traffic, and conversely if you are piloting a craft, be especially attentive for people in the water.

In the well over a century the Rhone *has been underwater, nature has transformed it from a sleek and, for her day, modern vessel into a bountiful reef. Sponges and hard corals adorn almost every surface of the wreck.*

sponges. This growth is delicate, so be especially careful with fins and gauges if you try to swim through the uprights. It is best to just keep back a bit and admire their exquisite beauty. Pinned under the wreck in front of the columns is one of the *Rhone*'s two cannons. The whereabouts of the other remains a mystery.

Continuing back towards the mast you'll pass two curved lifeboat davits, complete with pulleys and cleats. The wreck is slightly collapsed here, inviting you to explore the living reef growing on top. Fully developed coral heads and a carpet of flora and fauna would fool you into believing this is just another piece of sea floor, except for a giant open hatch and a line of gaping portholes, two with glass still intact.

The far end of the wreck is the long and graceful projection of the bow itself. On the now vertical foredeck are a massive stanchion post, the remains of the anchor windlass, and a huge iron ring. The ring used to contain the wooden bowsprit—a mammoth pole that projected forward of the ship and to which the foresails were attached.

Schools of yellowtail snapper ("*Rhone* piranha") will follow you throughout the dive. There are also several very friendly coneys and a magnificent pair of gray angelfish patrols the wreck. Eagle rays, turtles, big horse-eye jacks and the usual quota of beautiful reef fishes can also be seen. Alas, Abraham, a giant jewfish who befriended and overwhelmed many fortunate divers is now relegated to legend as he was apparently taken by fishermen a few years back.

Try to remember where your descent or mooring line is so that you can ascend slowly up the line directly to your boat. Don't forget to make a safety stop. Ascending without a line is asking for trouble. If the current is running, it can carry you away. Swimming on the surface with the amount of boat traffic on this site (a lot of it driven by weekend sailors in rent-a-boats) is downright dangerous.

The Stern Section. While the wreck is perfect for a two-dive tour with all new sights on the second dive, it is important that attention be paid to times and depths in order to avoid decompression complications. A minimum of a one hour surface interval is recommended before diving the stern section. Most boats reposition themselves between dives to be closer to the stern. There is a dinghy mooring tucked behind Black Rock that is perfect for this dive.

With a guide or conservative use of a computer, a planned step-dive can be undertaken which would permit visiting the mid and south sections at 65 feet (20 m). Otherwise, limit yourself to the remains of the stern section at a maximum depth of 45 feet (14 m). If you go for the full exploration, don't loiter on the wreckage under your boat, but do the deepest part of the dive first. Swim past the aft mast, which lies on the bottom pointing down the slope towards the mid section. Here there are two sets of columns or arches, as well as the remains of a massive winch and a set of huge open end wrenches lying on a rack. The "deep water" boiler sits near here, torn open by more recent storms. Out in the distance, deeper than is sensible to venture on this repetitive dive, is the boxy hulk of the condenser.

If air and bottom time permit, head south, skirting the deeper side of the other intact boiler and continue onto the south (or water pump) section. Here two sets of columns converge in a very dramatic way. If there's a current running, a school of large horse-eye jacks will hover above the uprights, allowing close scrutiny by the stealthy diver.

Spend the balance of the dive on the stern section itself. While not intact like the bow section, this is a fascinating area to explore. The shallower depth makes for a more leisurely pace and more color. The most obvious feature is the 70-foot-long (21 m) propeller shaft leading from the gear box housing up towards the shallowest end of the wreck. Inside the gear box housing are the "treasure chest" and a set of massive toothed gears. Near the other end of the shaft is the *Rhone*'s propeller. It makes up one end of a shallow swim-through under the very stern of the wreck. Strangely enough, divers often swim over this monster propeller, 15 feet (5 m) across, without noticing it—it's just that big. Directly behind the propeller is the huge rudder. Port holes abound, including one with most of its glass intact. Local legend has it that rubbing the brass will bring good luck, or at least keep the porthole shiny. The aft mast lies parallel to the wreck with chain and cable heaped over it. A ring at the end of the mast makes a nice frame for photography.

CHAPTER V VIRGIN GORDA

AT A GLANCE

The "Fat Virgin" slumbers peacefully at the far end of the Sir Francis Drake Channel. At first glance, Virgin Gorda appears to be less developed than Tortola, but look behind the palms and boulders, and you'll find a very upscale destination. A funky elegance pervades and many visitors have faithfully returned the same week every year for decades. In addition to the world renowned Little Dix Hotel, there are many other plush resorts and rental properties. Virgin Gorda, from the Baths on its southern tip to the yachtsman's playground in North Sound, is definitely a destination for the '90's.

The island is separated into two parts. The long, low southern section includes the Baths, Spanish Town and the Copper Mine. This area is quite dry, and scrub and cactus are common inshore. The northern half quickly rises 1,359 feet (412 m) to verdant Gorda Peak, and then spills over to Gorda Sound and the outlying islands that make up the North Sound area. A thin isthmus connects the two sections. The overall length is about ten miles (16 km) and with an area of approximately eight square miles (21 sq km), the island boasts a population of less than 2,500. Much of the island is undeveloped and protected as a National Park. There are enough beaches hidden in little bays and tucked into coves to keep even a passionate beachcomber occupied for several vacations.

Most visitors arrive by boat. There is limited air service to a small air strip on the east side. Ferries run several times a day from Road Town. Several times a week there is a direct run from the USVI, though you have to clear customs and immigration in Tortola first. The fast and sleek North Sound Express leaves from Trellis Bay near the airport on Beef Island. It connects with some of the flights from San Juan, and takes passengers to a number of stops in North Sound. Of course, if you're on your own boat you can come ashore most anywhere.

EXPLORING VIRGIN GORDA

Many day trippers visiting Virgin Gorda see only the Baths. Since they snorkel or dinghy directly ashore from a moored boat, they miss all the other attractions Virgin Gorda offers. The southern half of the island and Savannah Bay and Gorda Peak are easily explored from a car or taxi. But to really appreciate North Sound, it is necessary to travel by boat as many of the resorts and facilities are on offshore islands.

In times past, Spanish Town was briefly the capital of the BVI and it's now the most developed area of Virgin Gorda. This part of the island is called The Valley. The heart of it is the Virgin Gorda Yacht Harbour, home to Dive BVI, as well as many nautical and other businesses. The marina there is fully equipped and very popular, and the inter-island ferries land nearby.

A short distance from Spanish Town is Little Dix Bay Hotel. When Laurance Rockefeller built this resort in the 1960's it heralded the beginning of the tourist industry in the BVI. A stroll through the beautifully landscaped grounds shows what a large staff of dedicated gardeners can do. As the resort has recently undergone a multi-million dollar facelift, its continued place on various World's Top Ten

The Baths on the southern tip of Virgin Gorda are one of the most popular "day sail" destinations in the BVI. Beautiful beaches, huge boulders and interesting snorkeling all work to captivate the visitor.

Resorts lists is assured. The resort also owns the ferry dock, the marina, the airstrip and lots of land.

From Spanish Town it's easy to hail a taxi and begin your island tour. No trip to Virgin Gorda, or even the BVI, is complete without visiting the Baths. Driving south from Spanish Town you'll pass several resorts tucked into the shoreline (stop by later for cool drinks or a fine meal). As you near the Baths, the road winds its way around several huge house-sized boulders. In fact, several houses are built on top of or alongside these granite behemoths, often utilizing the natural stone as a fourth wall.

The National Parks Trust maintains a parking lot above the Baths. It's easy to make arrangements with your taxi driver to pick you up again at some prearranged time. The walk down through the boulders is a little tricky, and those heavily burdened with snorkel and beach apparatus had better watch their step. The most impressive way to approach the Baths is from the water. The huge gray boulders literally tumble down the green hills into the azure sea. The iridescent turquoise of the water is complemented by the golden glow of the beaches. The towering palms put it all into a tropical perspective. There are limited facilities at the Baths, including rest rooms, a T-shirt hawker and, of course, a beach bar.

Snorkeling off the Baths is great fun. Swimming through and exploring the pools and grottoes made by the boulders is a special treat. The reef structure is not overwhelming, but there is abundant fish life. A word of caution though: in winter when the Atlantic ground swell is up, there can be a dangerous surge running through the Baths, making swimming or even landing a dinghy a risky proposition.

The magic of the Baths lies in exploring its hidden recesses and dark pools, where the play of light dancing on the water is mesmerizing. Just south of the beach is the entrance, marked by a sign. A shuffling crab-walk through a narrow slot gains entrance to the wonderland. The first pool is the most famous. From there you can climb and slither your way up a series of rock faces to a summit of sorts. It can be slippery. A subtle trail continues in and around the boulders, through caves and pools, all the way to Devil's Bay. An afternoon spent exploring the Baths by foot

and snorkel is guaranteed to be a highlight of your vacation.

The Mad Dog Bar and the Top of the Baths sit above the Baths and are excellent places to watch the sunset and pick up the latest Virgin Gorda gossip. Between the Baths and Spanish Town are several other exquisite white sand beaches: Spring Bay, the Crawl and Valley Trunk Bay. The simplest access is by water, as some of the bordering land is privately owned.

From the Baths you can cut across the island to the southeastern corner, where Copper Mine Point juts out into the Atlantic. The ruins of an historic copper mine stand defiantly above the wave-swept rocky shore below. Tradition has it that the mine dates back to 16th century Spanish settlers. Copper ore was still being extracted by Cornish miners well into the 1800's. The most intact sections of the ruin are the tall stone chimney and adjacent boiler house. They are fairly delicate and not sturdy enough to be climbed on.

On the road along the narrow strip of land that connects the two halves of Virgin Gorda, there is a scenic pullover which offers an excellent view of the beautiful beaches of Savanna Bay and Tetor Bay. They are on the sheltered Caribbean side, whereas just up the road you'll see the sometimes turbulent Atlantic pounding against the cliffs of Red and Black Points.

From here the road curves up the side of Gorda Peak affording views of undeveloped South Sound. The National Parks Trust maintains a nature trail leading to the summit of Gorda Peak, the highest point on Virgin Gorda at 1,359 feet (412 m). This is an interesting hike as the area is home to many indigenous plants and has been reforested with mahogany. The Peak trail is one of the few places in the Virgins where the green of vegetation holds sway over the blue of the sea. There is a tower on the summit that offers an imposing view in all directions.

Continuing along the road, the huge expanse of North Sound comes into view and then the road quickly descends to sea level. North Sound is truly a yachtsman's playground, with plenty of fine anchorages, yacht-oriented resorts and protected sailing. The huge "lagoon" is ringed by islands and exquisite coral reefs. The road ends at Pusser's Leverick Bay Resort, a fun day destination, especially on weekends when there are scheduled activities.

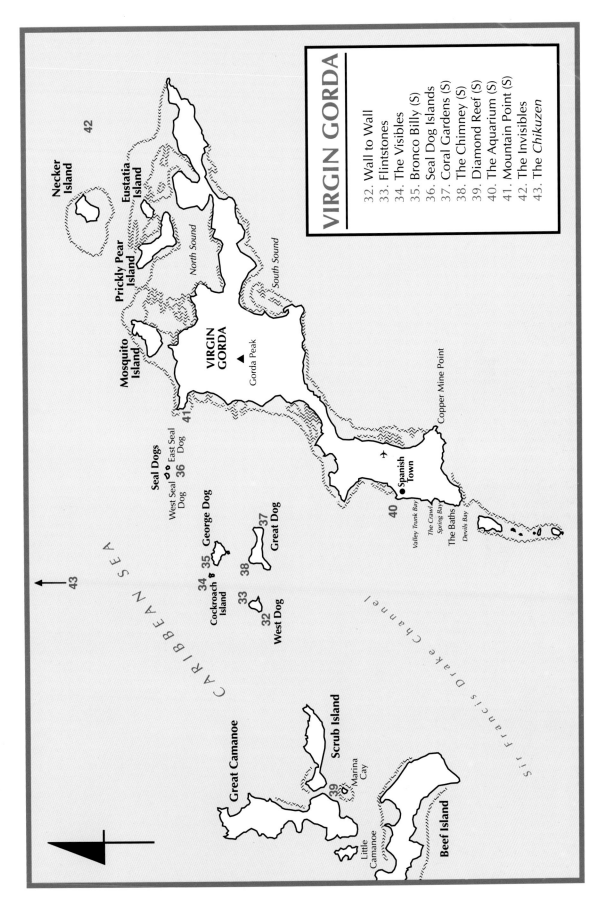

VIRGIN GORDA

32. Wall to Wall
33. Flintstones
34. The Visibles
35. Bronco Billy (S)
36. Seal Dog Islands
37. Coral Gardens (S)
38. The Chimney (S)
39. Diamond Reef (S)
40. The Aquarium (S)
41. Mountain Point (S)
42. The Invisibles
43. The *Chikuzen*

Necker Island

Eustatia Island

Prickly Pear Island

North Sound

South Sound

Mosquito Island

VIRGIN GORDA

▲ Gorda Peak

Copper Mine Point

Seal Dogs

West Seal Dog   East Seal Dog

George Dog

Great Dog

Cockroach Island

West Dog

CARIBBEAN SEA

Spanish Town

Valley Trunk Bay
The Crawl
Spring Bay
The Baths
Devils Bay

Great Camanoe

Scrub Island

Marina Cay

Sir Francis Drake Channel

Little Camanoe

Beef Island

It's also a convenient place to stay for a week of diving with Dive BVI and their on-site facility and dive boat.

Across the way is Mosquito Island (named after the Indians and not the bugs) and Drakes Anchorage, a long established resort on a private island. On the far side of North Sound is Prickly Pear Island, part of the National Parks. Vixen Point, on its southern tip, is a popular windsurfing and picnicking stop.

Attached to the eastern tip of Virgin Gorda is a long skinny peninsula that seems like a separate island, especially since it is not connected by road to the rest of the island. The huge Bitter End resort sits on this projection and makes up the eastern rim of North Sound. It's the turn-around point for most charters. In addition to a complete sailing and water sports facility, the Bitter End is the home base for Kilbride's Underwater Tours. The upscale Biras

Creek resort sits tucked back into a deep harbour near the Bitter End. It straddles a ridge and offers views and access to both sheltered North Sound and the open Atlantic. The restaurant is renowned for its fine cuisine.

Saba Rock, a tiny island nestled in between the Bitter End and Prickly Pear, is the site of the rather casual Pirates Pub & Grill, former home of Bert and Gayla Kilbride. Sailors and divers often stop by for a burger and a tall tale told by the charming and moderately eccentric Bert Kilbride, the BVI's unofficial old man of the sea.

Out past Eustacia Reef lies secluded Necker Island. The island is owned by Richard Branson of Virgin Atlantic Records and airline fame. He runs it as an exclusive resort right out of "life styles of the rich and famous." In fact it has been featured several times on that program, and guest book entries include

One of the few resorts in Virgin Gorda's North Sound accessible by car, Pusser's Leverick Bay attracts a lot of day visitors. Dive BVI operates a dive shop and boat from this location.

Part of the fun of exploring the unique natural wonder called the Baths is to venture in among the house-sized boulders. There is a trail that leads from pool to pool (the "baths" themselves) as well as over, under, around and through the boulders. This is the biggest pool and the first on the trail.

Princess Di and various Hollywood superstars.

Scattered across the end of the Sir Francis Drake Channel, just west of Virgin Gorda, are the Dogs, that wonderful collection of odd names and great dive sites. West Dog, Great Dog and George Dog are the largest, and then there's West Seal Dog and East Seal Dog, as well as Cockroach, one of our all time favorite BVI dives. These uninhabited islands have National Parks Trust Protected Area status.

WHERE TO STAY

If you're looking for on-site diving convenience, try Leverick Bay Resort, a full service resort in North Sound, with Dive BVI operating right on the premises, or the Bitter End and Kilbride's Diving Tours. For bigger budgets, world class Little Dix is an option, with on-site pickup by both Dive BVI and Kilbride's. There are the Guava Berry Spring Bay rental villas nestled in the boulders on the way to the Baths. Toad Hall is a very unusual holiday home located just above the Baths. In fact they have their own private boardwalk that meanders through the boulders right down to the beach. Fisher's Cove and The Olde Yard Inn are nice places as well. There are other rental houses in The Valley and scattered around North Sound.

Biras Creek, Drakes Anchorage, Leverick Bay and the Bitter End are all located in North Sound. They're top quality resorts offering fine food, comfortable accommodations and plenty of water-oriented activities. Biras is renowned for its cuisine and seclusion. Bitter End is the yacht-party center for the BVI. It's like a summer camp for adults, with its sprawling grounds and an active water sports center. Dive boats will pick up directly from all four resorts' docks.

Eat, Drink And Be Merry

While some consider Virgin Gorda to be even quieter than Tortola, there is in fact a very active island-style night life—you just have to know where to find it. There may be a band, a barbecue, or just a bunch of like-minded folk enjoying each other's company.

In the Yacht Harbour, try the Bath & Turtle, where most everyone passes through there sometime during the day. The Mad Dog and the new Top of the Baths overlooking the Baths, are great places to watch the sunset while enjoying a cold drink and a cool breeze. A little classier would be lunch or even dinner at Little Dix, or make it a special affair and dress up for a fantastic meal at Biras Creek. Also in North Sound are the Bitter End and Pusser's at Leverick Bay. Both offer fine food. You can drive to Pusser's (the Bitter End is accessible only by boat) and they frequently have some kind of fun theme night. We already mentioned the Kilbride's Pirates Pub on tiny Saba Rock. The Olde Yard Inn, Fischer's Cove, Chez Michelle, and Andy's Chateau de Pirate are other popular eateries. You can try more local style places, such as Anything Goes and Teacher Ilma's.

What To Do

Exploring Virgin Gorda (the Baths, the Copper Mine, Gorda Peak, North Sound) will certainly occupy much of your free time. In addition to shopping around Spanish Town, Leverick Bay and the Yacht Harbour, make sure you check out Little Dix, if only to dawdle in their gardens. Just south of the Yacht Harbour is Little Fort National Park, the remains of an old Spanish fort as well as a wildlife sanctuary.

Virgin Gorda excels in beaches, especially unique ones. In addition to the Baths-Devils Bay-The Crawl-Valley Trunk series of unforgettable beaches, don't miss Savannah Bay, Tetor Bay, as well as Prickly Pear in North Sound. There are many more, so be sure to ask your divemaster or hotel manager about their personal favorite.

You can also go sport fishing (out of Biras Creek), take sailing lessons or even rent a small boat (the Bitter End), and of course, day sail (Mirage Charters). Leverick Bay offers water skiing and windsurfing.

Diving And Dive Shops

The North Sound area of Virgin Gorda is certainly the water sports capital of the BVI; sailing, snorkeling, windsurfing and diving are all to be enjoyed in volume. While Eustacia and Colquhoun reef look especially inviting (and offer exceptional snorkeling), many of the established dive sites are situated around the various Dog Islands. The wreck of the *Chikuzen* is dived more from Virgin Gorda than from Tortola, but even from here it's weather dependent. The Virgin Gorda dive boats also dive some of the Tortola sites, often going to the Salt, Cooper and Ginger areas. There are two dive companies based in Virgin Gorda.

Dive BVI

Spanish Town & Leverick Bay

Dive BVI has two locations in Virgin Gorda: the Yacht Harbour in Spanish Town and Leverick Bay in North Sound. They also maintain a "dive person" at Little Dix Resort.

A PADI 5-Star Facility and a NAUI Dream Resort, Dive BVI offers dive tours and instruction at all their facilities, but considers Leverick Bay to be its dive education center. They offer a complete program of instruction from resort course all the way up to assistant instructor. Their dive boat from Leverick Bay picks up at all the North Sound resorts: Drake's Anchorage, Biras Creek and Bitter End.

The shop in Spanish Town is centrally located and handles the divers from that area. Their dive boat departs from in front of the shop in the Yacht Harbour. Both Dive BVI shops can arrange rendezvous diving and are well stocked with rental gear. They dive from Virgin Gorda all the way down to the *Rhone* at Salt Island. The wreck of the *Chikuzen* is scheduled once a week, weather permitting. They also make weekly snorkel trips to Anegada and other destinations.

Kilbride's Underwater Tours

Bitter End

Kilbride's Underwater Tours, located in Virgin Gorda's North Sound, is the oldest dive company in the BVI. Bert Kilbride started it over 20 years ago. He has since retired to his own tiny island, Saba Rock, and his Pirate's Pub. The dive shop is now on the dock at the Bitter End.

Kilbride's dive boat departs twice a day for nearby dive sites after picking up throughout the North Sound area. They can rendezvous with sailboats at various anchorages as well. They offer instruction from resort courses up to divemaster. Specialty courses as well as underwater videos of guests' dives are available. Their range is from the *Rhone* to the *Chikuzen*.

DIVE SITES

West Dog

32. WALL TO WALL

DEPTH:	15-65 FEET
	(5-20 M)
LEVEL:	ADVANCED
ACCESS:	BOAT
ANCHORAGE:	GREAT DOG

Wall to Wall, on the southwest corner of West Dog, was so named because the marine life there can be so abundant that sometimes it's just "wall to wall" with fish. Underneath the mooring is a sand patch surrounded by ledges and overhangs. Take the time at the beginning or end of the dive to thoroughly examine this area. Stretch out on the sand and peer deeply back into the coral and rock recesses looking for spotted rock lobster, juvenile angelfishes and lacy crinoids. There may even be a sleeping nurse shark tucked in, with just its tail sticking out or perhaps an octopus changing colors as it scurries along the reef. The corals here are healthy because they are spared the onslaught of the wintertime north swell.

To find the schools of fish, head out southwest, descending down the slope. There's a canyon that cuts through the slope, and a little deeper at 45 feet (14 m) or so, there are some boulders and more undercut ledges. This is where the "tons o' fish" are. Porkfish, blue striped grunts, squirrelfishes, bigeyes and even sergeant majors mill about this area. At times though, the schools aren't so plentiful and it's not quite "wall to wall," but only "wall...."

33. FLINTSTONES

DEPTH:	40-70 FEET
	(12-21 M)
LEVEL:	INTERMEDIATE
	TO ADVANCED
ACCESS:	BOAT
ANCHORAGE:	GREAT DOG

Because of the prevailing wind, the mooring at this site on the north side of West Dog tends to put you pretty far offshore. Beneath the boat, in about 70 feet (21 m) of water, is a sandy area. The corals around here are a little stunted due to the site's exposure to the north swell. When the swell is really up, the resultant surge just tears at the bottom and only the hardiest marine life can survive. Look around here for big southern stingrays and maybe some nurse sharks before heading up the slope to the main attraction.

Scattered along the bottom, in 40 to 50 feet (12-15 m) of water, is a series of huge boulders. These massive rocks are the bedrock that gives the site its name. They form a network of ledges, overhangs and hollows which are filled with fishes. Working your way east, you'll come across Fred's Rock, a huge house-sized boulder rising up from 65 feet (20 m). Beneath an overhang on this behemoth is a shadowy den filled with fishes. Smallmouth grunts, fairy basslets and sergeant majors all compete for space.

Caution. While Flintstones is not subject to strong currents, it is exposed to the full brunt of the north swell when it is up (generally in winter). So if the swell is running, don't dive here.

Cockroach

34. THE VISIBLES

DEPTH:	10-80 FEET
	(3-24 M)
LEVEL:	ADVANCED
ACCESS:	BOAT
ANCHORAGE:	GEORGE DOG

The Visibles is one of the authors' favorite BVI dives. While strong currents often buffet the site there is always a lot of life here (some of it rather large) and the topography is simply spectacular. An entire action-packed dive can be spent in slow circumnavigation of this "sea mount."

The NPT mooring is set into a pinnacle that sits about 100 yards (91 m) off the southwestern tip of Cockroach Island. The pinnacle comes within a dozen feet (4 m) of the surface and is visible from a boat. It is recommended that you ascend and descend on the mooring line or on your own weighted descent line, otherwise the current is apt to pull you away from the site. Once down, stop and regroup in the protective lee of the pinnacle before going out into the tumult. And what a tumult it is. If you work your way along the ridge towards shore, you'll encounter a series of huge coral- and sponge-encrusted boulders, including an immense overhang filled with fishes. A large barracuda has staked out the top of the pinnacle and he yields his territory very begrudgingly. Head south through a pass between the rocks and you'll come out onto a sloping wall that will be swept by the current if it's running. This slope is thick with huge deep-water gorgonians, luxuriant sea fans and lots of fish life. Swim to your right (west), dropping down along the face of the slope as you go. As you get deeper and out towards the tip, the current will push you along. Look out into open water for eagle rays, turtles, sharks and large pelagic fishes. Sometimes, if they're heading into the current, they'll be slowed down enough to afford a lingering view.

At the point, at about 80 feet (24 m), there is a series of ledges and then large overhangs and little caves as you come around the corner and head shallower. This area is just overflowing with fish life. There is a huge school of ghost-like bigeyes that drifts out among the boulders (similar to the glasseye snappers that hide under ledges). Highhats, angelfishes and large snappers loiter in this area. It is an exciting place. You get the feeling that anything might swim by, but you'll probably miss it because you'll be buried up to your knees poking around under one of the ledges. Continue up along the other side of the pinnacle/ridge making sure that you don't overstay your time at depth. You should end up underneath your boat.

Up in the shallows next to the island, there is a fantastic maze of alleyways, tunnels, arches and monster boulders all covered with encrusting sponges, corals, hydroids and lots of fire coral. It's a long swim across a current-swept plain to get from the mooring to the shallows, but if you have lots of air (or are doing a second dive here) it's definitely worth exploring. You can play hide and seek with queen angelfish, trumpetfish and masses of sergeant majors.

Snorkeling. Snorkeling in the shallows when conditions are calm should be attempted only by advanced snorkelers, but beware of the current.

George Dog

35. BRONCO BILLY (S)

DEPTH:	15-50 FEET
	(5-15 M)
LEVEL:	NOVICE
	TO ADVANCED
ACCESS:	BOAT
ANCHORAGE:	THE SITE; LEE OF
	GEORGE DOG

Bronco Billy is a popular Dogs dive, especially for those yearning for something a little more exciting than Coral Gardens or the Chimney, but still wanting a relatively easy dive. Situated at the northwestern tip of George Dog, Bronco Billy offers a meandering course of coral ridges

The uninhabited Dog Islands off Virgin Gorda enjoy protected status as part of BVI National Parks Trust. George Dog, with Great Dog in the background, are nesting sites for sea birds as well as the locations for some of Virgin Gorda's best diving: the Chimney, Bronco Billy and the Visibles (off Cockroach).

and corresponding canyons.

From the moorings, head north and you should encounter one of two coral archways leading into the canyons. Follow the canyons and the bottom topography around the tip of George Dog into a large steep-walled box canyon and boulder field. Swing a little wider around the tip of the island on your return trip, and you should find the other coral canyon that will lead you back to the second archway and your boat.

Large pillar coral formations grace the site, but the highlight is the arches. When lit with a diver's flashlight or a photographer's strobe the colors just explode. The brilliant reds of the encrusting sponges and the oranges of the cup corals, combining with the lavender of other sponges and the lacy frill of hydroids, makes for a Technicolor extravaganza. However, without a light or strobe there is nothing there but shadow and muted colors.

Snorkeling. Snorkeling along the shore from the orange mooring is suggested for the experienced, and only when conditions permit.

Caution. Again, like most other Dogs dives, when the north swell is up the resulting surge makes this an uncomfortable, if not dangerous, dive. In fact, the site was named Bronco Billy because the surge in the box canyon can give you a ride like a bucking bronco. Novice divers can dive this site when conditions are calm, but entering the swim-throughs or diving in surge should best be left to advanced divers.

The spotted cleaner shrimp is one of several species of small shrimps and fishes that establish cleaning stations. The shrimp advertises its services by crawling out onto the tips of the anemone's tentacles and waving its antennae. Larger fishes come to be cleaned of dead skin and small parasites.

Deep inside the shadows of a small cave, two tiny gobies perch atop a small sponge formation. The bright colors of the sponge are visible only under artificial light—such as a dive light or a photographer's strobe.

36. SEAL DOG ISLANDS

DEPTH:	20-60 FEET (6-18 M)
LEVEL:	ADVANCED
ACCESS:	BOAT
ANCHORAGE:	GREAT OR GEORGE DOG

The small companion islands of West Seal Dog and East Seal Dog mark the far end of the Sir Francis Drake Channel. Just past these two tiny sentinels, the Caribbean Sea becomes the Atlantic Ocean. The NPT mooring is off the southwest corner of West Seal Dog. There is some protection from the north, but if the ground sea is up in winter, it is advisable to choose another more protected site.

While there is a shallow saddle between the two Seal Dogs, the best part of the site is along the western side of West Seal Dog. The bottom beneath the mooring is around 25 feet (8 m), from there head west, away from the island, down the slope to about 70 feet (21 m). Pause here to look around for large pelagic fish passing through from the open Atlantic. Jacks, mackerel, kingfish and perhaps an eagle ray or two might promenade by.

Turn right (north) and maintain a fixed depth for a while as you parallel the west side of the island. Before you go too far and use up all your air, head back up the slope to the shallows for the highlight of the dive. Along the bottom of the cliff off the northwest side of the island are fantastic rock formations made up of monster boulders and the convoluted bedrock of the island itself. Take the time to explore the myriad of canyons, swim-throughs, ledges and tiny caves. Remember you have to return to the mooring around the corner.

There is a breaking rock just to the northeast of the two Seal Dog Islands, called Seal Dog Rock. The dive is a circumnavigation of the rock exploring the steep walls and looking out into the blue for passing pelagics. It is an exciting place to be, perched on a pinnacle situated on the edge of the Virgin Islands. This is most definitely an advanced dive due to its complete lack of protection and moderate to deeper depths on the far side.

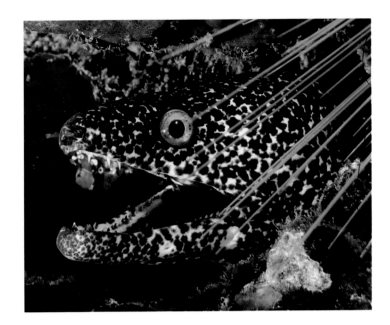

Contrary to its portrayal in popular literature, the moray eel is a shy and retiring creature. If approached too closely, it will retreat. In fact, far more divers are hurt by urchin spines, which this spotted eel is hiding behind, than by morays.

Great Dog

37. CORAL GARDENS (AIRPLANE WRECK) (S)

DEPTH:	20-50 FEET
	(6-15 M)
LEVEL:	NOVICE
ACCESS:	BOAT
ANCHORAGE:	TRELLIS BAY;
	SPANISH TOWN

Coral Gardens is a nice quiet dive site tucked into the eastern tip of the south side of Great Dog. As befitting such a popular spot, the National Parks Trust has installed enough moorings so that interested divers rarely have to wait for another group to depart. As the name suggests, Coral Gardens boasts large beautiful coral formations. These consist primarily of mounds of boulder star coral and great star coral, well embellished with brain corals, tube sponges, sea fans and gorgonians. Under the overhangs look for lobsters, spotted drums and assorted grunts and snappers.

To the east of the moorings is a large sand patch. Out on the sand stingrays, schools of sennet, occasional turtles and blacktip sharks, as well as the very unusual flying gurnard have been seen. Otherwise, count on goatfish, lizardfishes and sand tilefish.

A recent addition to the dive site is the remains of Atlantic Air BVI's Shorts 360 airplane. In 1993, after making an abortive take off, their one and only aircraft landed in the water about 200 feet (61 m) off the end of the runway. No one was hurt, but after the airplane was refloated from 30 feet (9 m) of water it languished hidden in a hangar for many months before being used as a movie prop in a BBC film. It eventually found its way out to Great Dog where it was sunk as part of the BVI's continual artificial reef program. The plane, without wings or tail, sits in the sand patch in about 40 feet (12 m) of water. It's easy to find; just follow the shore side of the patch until you see it. One wonders about the Heineken bottle found wedged behind the pilot's seat—just kidding!

Due to its location on the south side of Great Dog, Coral Gardens is more sheltered from the occasional wintertime north swell than many of the other Dogs area sites. However, it is exposed to sea conditions coming from the south. It is also a popular night dive site, with puffers, sleeping parrotfishes, and foraging squirrelfishes to be seen.

38. THE CHIMNEY (S)

DEPTH:	15-45 FEET
	(5-14 M)
LEVEL:	NOVICE (WITH
	GUIDE)
ACCESS:	BOAT
ANCHORAGE:	ON SITE

This is the most popular dive in the Virgin Gorda/Dogs area, and rivals the *Rhone* and the Indians in diver satisfaction. Tucked into the northern corner of the bay on the western side of Great Dog, the Chimney is really two sites in one. Under the NPT moorings is the Fish Bowl, where many a novice has first experienced the joys of scuba diving. A little further on, concealed in the meandering ridges at the point, is the famous Chimney, reputed to be the favorite BVI dive of none other than Jacques Yves Cousteau himself, because of the unusual white sponges that adorn the walls.

Directly below the moorings, in 30 to 40 feet (9-12 m) of calm protected water, are several massive coral heads rising up from a sand and rubble bottom. This is the Fish Bowl, so named because of the many friendly fishes abiding here. The yellowtails, sergeant majors, parrotfishes and other fishes have been fed by

so many divers that, just like Pavlov's dogs, they are conditioned to the sound of Velcro. Open a BC pocket, and zoom, you'll be surrounded by a mass of finny mouths all looking for a handout. This is a great spot for new divers and many of the local dive operators bring their resort or introductory course students here for their first dive.

Caution. If the north swell is up, there can be a strong surge at this site, however, this is primarily a wintertime problem.

To find the Chimney pass through the Fish Bowl heading towards the northern shore of the bay. Take the time to explore the several canyons and ridges that run parallel to shore. Work your way around the point. At a depth of around 45 feet (14 m) or so, cut back (to your right) and follow a canyon back towards shore. This should lead you under a large beautifully encrusted archway. Close examination of the underside of the arch will disclose a dense encrustation of cup corals and brightly colored sponges. Once through the arch you'll enter a steep-walled narrow corridor which ends with two huge rocks almost touching. The narrow slot between these two boulders is the Chimney, so named because of its resemblance to a rock-climbing formation of the same name. Before exiting through the slot take the time to look around at all the marine life on the walls. A dive light will reveal all the brilliant hues and hidden creatures—little shrimp, spotted rock lobster, anemones and a

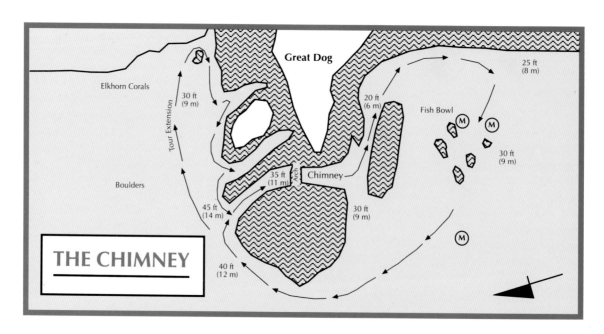

rainbow of sponges. Of special note are the unusual white sponges adorning the walls, which, says one local wag, resemble wads of chewing gum. If the Chimney slot looks too narrow for you, it is possible to swim out over the top of it. Be sure to watch your buoyancy as you'll be quite close to the surface. Once through the Chimney there are a couple of canyons along the cliff face worth exploring as you work your way back through the Fish Bowl to your mooring.

Caution. If there is a north swell running, the Chimney itself can be a dangerous place to be because of the amplified effect of the surge in the narrow canyon. In such conditions, not only can you hurt yourself, but it is difficult not to damage the delicate marine growth with fin blades and tanks as you're being tossed about.

If you're a slow breather or have dived this site before, think about continuing further around the point before turning back to come through the arch and chimney. There are lots of less visited canyons and rock formations hidden there. You can also explore the base of the cliff further back into the bay. The bottom is covered with stones rubbed round and smooth from years of rolling in the winter surge. Among these stones is a wealth of tiny marine creatures such as brittle stars, baby flame scallops and an occasional scorpionfish. This is also an excellent place to snorkel.

Nestled into the west side of Great Dog Island, the Chimney is an excellent dive site. The Chimney itself is visible in the bottom center of the picture. The snorkeling is outstanding all along the rocky shore.

39. DIAMOND REEF (S)

DEPTH:	10-35 FEET
	(3-11 M)
LEVEL:	NOVICE
ACCESS:	BOAT
ANCHORAGE:	MARINA CAY

Diamond Reef probably isn't on anyone's top ten list, but it is a friendly little reef just right for brand new divers or snorkelers, and perfect for a quiet afternoon spent puttering around underwater. It is an exquisite night dive.

Located on the southeast side of Great Camanoe, Diamond Reef is usually dived from Marina Cay. There is no mooring here so dinghy over and carefully anchor on the reef shallows, north of the small dock on Camanoe. A larger boat should anchor in the sand channel. Start your dive along the bottom of the reef, heading north along the mini-wall towards Scrub Island. Out in the sand, adjacent to the reef, is a colony of garden eels. These often-overlooked residents of the sand flats look like a field of sea grass waving in the breeze. Just the head and upper body of these pencil-thin eels protrudes from a permanent burrow. Approach too closely and they will, almost imperceptibly, slip back into their

Like its cousins the nudibranchs, the lettuce sea slug is basically a snail-without-a-shell. It is a vegetarian, feeding on algae (and even storing fully functioning chloroplasts stolen from its algae prey in the ruffles on its back). True nudibranchs are carnivores, feeding on hydroids, sponges and other animals.

burrows and disappear.

Take advantage of the fact that this reef slopes down to a sand bottom. Stretch out on the sand and crawl right up to the coral for an intimate and prolonged observation of all the tiny creatures inhabiting a single coral head. You can get within inches of the coral without touching or damaging it by coming in slowly on the sand. After you've ambled down the reef for a while return to your boat along the top of the reef, looking for blue chromis, tiny wrasses and parrotfishes.

Virgin Gorda

40. THE AQUARIUM (S)

DEPTH:	15-30 FEET
	(5-9 M)
LEVEL:	NOVICE
ACCESS:	BOAT
ANCHORAGE:	SPANISH TOWN;
	THE BATHS;
	VALLEY TRUNK
	BAY

The rest of your gang is off shopping in Spanish Town or headed back to the Baths again, and you're dying for a dive. Well, just between town and the Baths is a shallow shoal of a reef (called Fischer's Rocks on some charts) that is very pretty indeed. Pillar coral formations, shy schools of French grunts and moray eels tucked under ledges await you.

While not as exciting as some of the premier sites, the Aquarium offers a very rewarding dive for both new divers or snorkelers, and experienced fish watchers. It's not a large site, but a slow circumnavigation and thorough exploration of the reef should use up a tank. Once off the reef there's not much other than plains of waving gorgonians. The Aquarium is rather densely textured with lots of rocks and boulders piled up on one another creating a network of small grottos and dens filled with fishes. Sergeant majors, blue tang and chromis fill the mid-water region. Sponges, fire coral and various crawling invertebrates cover the

rocks. Nurse sharks can be found napping under the larger ledges.

Caution. Due to the shallow depths and the large amount of boat traffic (both silent sailboats and fast speedboats), be especially aware of your buoyancy control, as you don't want to inadvertently float to the surface here.

41. MOUNTAIN POINT (S)

DEPTH:	20-70 FEET
	(6-21 M)
LEVEL:	NOVICE
ACCESS:	BOAT
ANCHORAGE:	LONG BAY

Lying outside the Anguilla Point entrance to North Sound, Mountain Point juts out into the Sir Francis Drake Channel, defining its western extreme. The rocky ridge of this point breaks apart as it projects out into the water, resulting in several cuts through the ridge, one called the "cow's mouth."

There are three NPT moorings on the sheltered, western side of the point. The two moorings located further back are over companion sites called the Jacuzzi and Paul's Grotto. Mountain Point, the site described here, is dived by picking up the buoy closest to the point, in about 35 feet (11 m) of water. Large coral heads, overhangs and sand patches are the basic reef structure here. Grunts, parrotfishes and butterflyfishes are common. Look for lizardfishes in and around the sand patches. In the summertime large tarpon can be seen sweeping through the huge schools of tiny fry. Novices, especially without a dive guide should stay in this area (on the west side of the point), or they can work their way along the shoreline, back towards the other NPT moorings. There are some caves and large bowls or grottos in the bedrock. Be careful of surge in the shallows.

Experienced divers can venture through the "cow's mouth," exploring the narrow cut between the rock formations. Once on the other side head down the steep slope. There is generally more action here. Large jacks, barracudas and maybe a ray are possible passersby. There is a colony of garden eels in the sand here. Make sure you have enough air remaining to make your way back through the cut to your boat.

Snorkeling should only be attempted in calm conditions by experienced snorkelers.

42. THE INVISIBLES

DEPTH:	15-65 FEET
	(5-20 M)
LEVEL:	ADVANCED
ACCESS:	BOAT
ANCHORAGE:	NONE

The Invisibles are perched at the end of the Virgin Islands, north of Virgin Gorda and east of Necker Island. The Atlantic Ocean and Anegada's treacherous Horse Shoe Reef are all that lie beyond. A trip out here is a special treat, promising encounters with large marine life. Due to its very remote location and exposure to the open ocean, this site is rarely dived. It is also difficult to locate—just getting past the reefs surrounding North Sound is a challenge. So your best and safest bet is to dive the Invisibles with one of the local dive shops when they schedule a trip in the summer. On a calm day the summit of the Invisibles lies just below the surface. But if there is any kind of sea, the waves will break as they roll over the rock, and the shallows will be obscured by froth and foam. The NPT mooring is located just southeast of the twin pinnacles. Wind shifts and currents can conspire to swing the boat onto the rocks, so be aware.

It isn't too difficult to swim around the formation on one dive. From the mooring, head to the rocks and you'll see a saddle between the two peaks. This area is piled high with rocks and boulders. There are a couple of swim throughs and overhangs worth exploring. Be careful of the surge if there is any kind of swell overhead. Continuing around the outside of the formation, you'll find a large overhang sheltering fishes from the marauding predators that come in from the open sea. Durgons, grunts, hinds and smaller tropicals can be found here. On the far side of the pinnacle the bottom slopes gradually away to 70 feet (21 m) or more. The visibility is usually pretty good,

80 to 100 feet (24-30 m) or more. If you pause here and look out into the blue, you never know what might cruise by. Certainly schools of horse-eye jacks and solitary mackerel are to be expected, but eagle rays, large permit, milling schools of spadefish and occasional sharks are often seen as well.

43. THE *CHIKUZEN*

DEPTH:	45-80 FEET
	(14-24 M)
LEVEL:	ADVANCED
ACCESS:	BOAT
ANCHORAGE:	NONE

Halfway to Anegada, out in the middle of the Atlantic Ocean, lies one of the BVI's most exciting dives, the wreck of the *Chikuzen*. There is no mooring to mark the site.

One fine August morning in 1981, the 246-foot (75 m) *Chikuzen* drifted like a ghost ship into the BVI. It had been abandoned—not a living soul was aboard. Smoldering fires produced a thick plume of smoke. The local authorities were content to let it drift right through, but when it threatened to run up on Marina Cay they were forced into action. Eventually a sea-going tug from St. Croix took the hulk under tow. At this point no one knew who owned the ship or where it had come from, or for that matter, who was going to pay for the tow. When the tow line snapped and the recoiling line shattered a crewman's legs, it was the last straw. That night the *Chikuzen* sank in 80 feet (24 m) of water out in open ocean.

It turned out the *Chikuzen* was a decrepit Japanese refrigeration vessel, part of a fishing fleet based in St. Marten. When a storm had threatened the leeward islands, the St. Marten Harbour Master demanded that the immobile *Chikuzen* be moved from the pier so it wouldn't destroy the docks. The owners towed the ship out to sea and tried to scuttle her. They set her on fire, but she didn't sink. Abandoned, she drifted to the BVI.

Today the ship lies on her port side. The starboard rail comes within 45 feet (14 m) of the surface. A huge multi-blade propeller marks the stern. The bow has dramatic railings, large winches and one of the ship's anchors. Projecting from the main deck are two massive masts, sticking out roughly parallel to the sea floor. These masts, used as loading cranes, are covered with heavy rigging and festooned with encrusting sponges. Most of the superstructure has fallen off and lies in a twisted jumble next to the ship. The ship itself is covered with oysters, sea squirts, sponges, gorgonian soft corals and small colonies of hard corals. The two refrigeration holds are easily accessible, but it is quite dangerous inside. The miles of tubing once used for cooling are slowly breaking loose, and their instability creates a safety hazard.

The surrounding terrain in all directions is a barren sand bottom, an underwater desert, so the wreck acts as an oasis for fishes. Immediately upon sinking, the *Chikuzen* became an artificial reef, a magnet attracting marine life. Thick clouds of fishes cover the wreck. Masses of gray snapper ebb and flow over the ship like the waves above. Barracudas fill the space between the ship and the surface. They're stacked like cord wood and every year they get bigger. Shark-like cobia occasionally patrol the wreck or lie on the sand bottom, propped up on their pectoral fins. Two jewfish are often seen, usually disappearing into the treacherous bowels of the ship.

Huge stingrays can be spotted buried up to their eyeballs in the fine white sand surrounding the wreck. A slow cautious approach will often result in an eyeball-to-eyeball encounter. If you're especially quiet and think only good thoughts, sometimes you can gently pet their velvety skin. Remember, these aren't the "paid" lap dogs you've seen elsewhere, but majestic wild animals condescending to let you approach.

Sharks are sometimes spotted on the fringes of the wreck, but they usually zoom away as soon as they see you. Now and again, thick schools of spadefish sweep down and encircle a diver before moving off. Large amberjack can be enticed to come in close by rapid dizzying swirling—the more active you are, the closer they come in. Horse-eye jacks can school in the hundreds. A pair of friendly gray angelfish like to admire themselves in the lenses of underwater cameras. A few years back two divers were treated to a sight they'll

The massive winch on the foredeck of the Chikuzen *is one of many recognizable features of this wreck, which sank in open ocean in 1981. But the real attraction is the enormous number of fishes that call this offshore wreck home.*

never forget. They watched in jaw-dropped awe as a mature humpback whale circled the wreck twice and then glided into the blue.

Caution. When the sea conditions and fish life cooperate, the *Chikuzen* is as good as it gets. However, if there is a swell running (and sometimes it's hard to notice it in open ocean), conditions on the site deteriorate to dangerous. The surge, as it rolls into the wreck, kicks up the sand and visibility drops to nothing. The movement of surge is amplified and you can get pushed back and forth by the surge further than you can see—not safe. Other hazards include the temptation to stay down too long, especially on the second dive. It's easy to stray off the wreck and get lost on the featureless plain; currents can complicate this even more. It's best to dive this site on a calm day with a commercial operator.

CHAPTER **VI**   ANEGADA

AT A GLANCE

Since the days of the Spanish Main, the 40-mile-wide (65 km) Anegada Passage has been one of the principal channels for entering and exiting the Caribbean from the Atlantic. Vessels following this route face a terrible danger: foundering on the coral-encircled island of Anegada or tearing their bottoms open on Horse Shoe Reef, an 18-mile-long (29 km) shoal of jagged coral which extends 10 miles (16 km) southeast of the island and lies hidden just below the surface. Since mariners have kept count, this low island and its treacherous reef have claimed over 300 vessels.

Unlike its neighbors which are primarily volcanic in origin, Anegada is a flat coral and limestone atoll, fringed with mile after mile of deserted beach. It is the second largest island in the territory, with a mass of 15 square miles (39 sq km) and dimensions of roughly 10 by 2-1/2 miles (16x4 km). With a maximum elevation of only 28 feet (9 m), the island sits low on the horizon, barely visible to passing ships. There are only about 160 inhabitants. Its unique geography, sparse population and remoteness from the rest of the BVI, really make Anegada a world unto itself.

In days past, the cry of "vessel on the reef" brought out small boats of every description. The islanders rushed to be first to the ship in distress. Their motives were not always humanitarian. And if wrecks failed to occur in the natural course of events, there were those who helped bring them about through falsely placed lights and other means. Pirates also occupied the island, thinking that the maze of reefs placed them beyond pursuit. Legends of lost treasure still persist.

The colorful and dangerous pirates from the days of sail are long gone, and Anegada is now inhabited by friendly folk who fish for a living.

Conch, lobsters and small reef fishes are harvested. There is a small simple resort hotel catering to visiting yachtsman and divers, and miles of deserted white sand beaches for those who want to get away from it all. But the hazards of Horse Shoe Reef remain and many a modern vessel lies beneath the foaming surf alongside the ancient wrecks. Most charter companies place Anegada off-limits to their charterers because of these dangers.

EXPLORING ANEGADA

From the air, the sunken and desolate nature of Anegada is quite obvious, as most of the interior is either underwater or covered by thorn bush. Two massive salt ponds lie in the interior of the western half of the island and another on the eastern tip. The ponds and the generally low elevation of the island give rise to Anegada's nickname: the sunken island. In fact, the word Anegada actually means "drowned land." In one of Anegada's mysterious twists, freshwater rises up to the surface of the land through natural springs.

Visitors generally arrive by sea, coming in by boat through the shoals and numerous coral heads to the west end of the island. It is also possible to fly there via scheduled flights on Gorda Aero or on a charter flight on Fly BVI. During the brief flight from Beef Island Airport you'll be treated to a bird's-eye view of the beauty and treachery of Horse Shoe Reef. There are roads of sorts running around the western half of the island, connecting the airstrip, the Settlement (where most of the islanders reside), the north beaches and the tourist facilities around Setting Point. Most

Anegada is known for its friendly people and excellent seafood. The Big Bamboo at Loblolly Bay is a favorite lunch spot.

people start their island exploration at Lowell Wheatley's Anegada Reef Hotel at Setting Point, where the staff will only be too happy to assist with information, directions and car rentals.

From here, head west on the south shore road to the beaches starting at Pomato Point. The road, a sand track really, gets a little complicated at the West End, but by doubling back a bit you should be able to find the road to the north shore. This is a beautiful drive winding from beach to salt pond.

Re-introduced flamingos inhabit one of the salt ponds. They might survive this time, if the locals can be convinced that the birds are more valuable in the wild than on the barbecue. The rare Anegada rock iguana lives only in Anegada, near Bones Bight. It is listed as highly endangered. A small number were recently transferred to Guana Island (in exchange for the flamingos) to protect the species against local disaster. A sighting of this massive lizard is quite a privilege and doesn't come easily. There are also wild orchids and, of course, miles of empty beaches.

The main road cuts back towards the airstrip before heading north again to Loblolly Bay. There is a track that continues along the north shore, but it's four wheel at best. Be careful of soft sand and sinking in the swampy areas. When you're done at Loblolly, come back by the airstrip again, get on the one paved road and visit the Settlement. You should make it back to the Reef Hotel just in time for sunset and a cold drink.

WHERE TO STAY

Anegada Reef Hotel has long been the place to stay and eat on Anegada, but it's not the

Battered by winter waves, Anegada's Horse Shoe Reef extends for miles past the sunken island's East End. Over the centuries hundreds of ships have foundered on this treacherous coral reef.

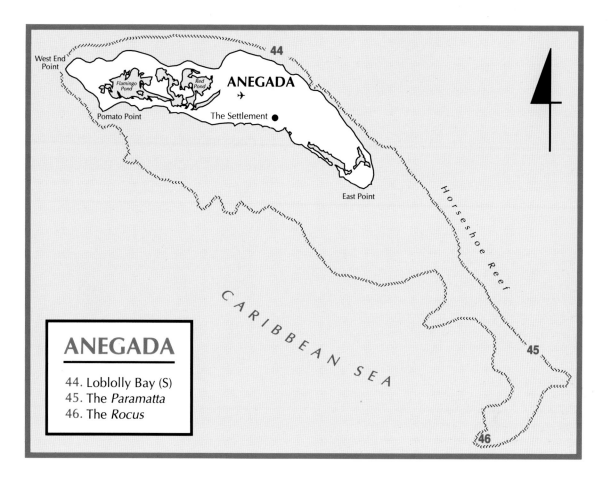

only one. There's also a campground at Neptune's Treasure, just up the road from the Hotel. A few rental cottages are also available. The Ocean Range guest house in the Settlement is an affordable alternative. As Anegada becomes more "discovered," there will be even more options.

Eat, Drink And Be Merry

There aren't too many options and most folk end up at the Anegada Reef Hotel for dinner. Lowell's barbecued lobster and rum smoothies are legendary. Nearby Neptune's Treasure offers dining, along with a campground. Check out Pam's Kitchen for fresh baked sweets and locally made jams and sauces. There's also a restaurant and a museum (a few interesting Arawak artifacts and shipwreck booty) at Pomato Point, where the beaches start in earnest. On the north side, there's the Big Bamboo at Loblolly Bay. Since you're going to end up there anyway, why not do it for lunch. An après-snorkel meal of barbecue lobster, washed down with Aubrey's famous Rum

Teaser is just what your therapist ordered. There are also a few places to eat in the Settlement.

What To Do

Rental jeeps, bicycles and taxi tours are available. A quick tour of the island is easily done in half a day. Most people come to Anegada for its beaches and the remoteness. You can walk forever on the north shore beaches. Protected by the offshore barrier reef, these beaches offer fine shell hunting and snorkeling. The best known is Loblolly.

You can also go sport fishing out in the Atlantic or bonefishing on the flats off the south shore. With a boat and a guide (navigating the reef necessitates this), exploring, snorkeling and perhaps diving the reef is open to you. On a day trip (by air) from Tortola we would recommend you forgo scuba and spend the day exploring the island and simply snorkel at Loblolly.

FISHERIES PROTECTED AREA

In 1990 the Department of Conservation and Fisheries established a Fisheries Protected Area that encompassed most of Horse Shoe Reef. It was marked with buoys the next year. There is no anchoring or fishing permitted in the area. While it hasn't been strictly closed to divers, the no-anchor policy has made it extremely difficult for divers to actually dive Horseshoe Reef sites. Furthermore, the Department of Conservation requested that the dive shops abstain from diving there.

It is proposed to open certain parts of the reef to local commercial fishermen, but to maintain the no-anchoring policy forever. The dive companies, Conservation and National Parks Trust are trying to work together to establish guidelines and a mooring system that works for all and still protects the unique ecosystem of Horseshoe Reef.

DIVING AND DIVE SHOPS

There are no full service dive shops on Anegada. Lowell at Anegada Reef Hotel usually maintains a compressor and a few tanks for shore dives at Loblolly. He suggests that if it's rough, just snorkel instead. Due to the lack of moorings and the treacherous nature of the reef, it's best to work with an experienced dive shop or charter skipper when trying to dive the wrecks.

Twenty miles (32 km) of virgin barrier reef ...Pirates ... Spanish treasure ... 300 shipwrecks. It all sounds like a diver's fantasy come true. The reality is a little different. Due to Horse Shoe Reef's location, stretching out into the open Atlantic Ocean, and its shallow depths, the majority of the coral is compact and stubby. Because the reef is pounded by winter waves, only the hardiest corals thrive. It's not the intricate swaying coral jungle you might imagine, though there are magnificent stands of elkhorn coral and oversized boulder coral formations. And while there are 300 recorded shipwrecks, the majority are so old that their wooden timbers have long since rotted away and their contents spread across acres of ocean floor. However, it's not as gloomy as all that, for there are a handful of relatively intact modern steel shipwrecks to explore and parts of the reef are quite beautiful. And you never know when you

might stumble across part of the famed Anegada treasure. Many have looked for it. The gold doubloon hanging around Bert Kilbride's neck had to come from somewhere.

DIVE SITES

44. LOBLOLLY BAY (S)

DEPTH:	5-40 FEET
	(2-12 M)
LEVEL:	ADVANCED
ACCESS:	BEACH
ANCHORAGE:	ANEGADA

Loblolly Bay is on the north shore of Anegada, tucked in behind the protective barrier of Horse Shoe Reef. Just offshore, the open-ocean waves of the Atlantic Ocean roll in and crash on the outer crest of the reef. By the time the waves reach the beautiful white sand of Loblolly, they've been reduced to a gentle lapping. This is a beach dive as no boat can get through the reef. Tanks are available on the island (or if you're on a charter boat you might have your own) and it's not a big deal to bring them to the beach by taxi or rental car.

Excellent snorkeling. The snorkeling here is great, and even if you may not be able to loiter on the bottom while breath-hold diving, you certainly can skim over the reef shallows with an ease that makes a tank-toting diver envious.

You can see the reef structure clearly. The dark color of the coral contrasts with the sparkling blue of the sun-dappled sandy shallows and the darker indigo blue indicates where the deep holes are. Just beyond is the brilliant white of the breaking surf. Enter the water just to the west of the Big Bamboo Bar/Restaurant. As you swim out over the "barren" sand look for schools of mojarra flitting around the bottom and needlefishes skimming just below the surface. In the sand are scores of holes inhabited by mantis shrimp and other assorted creatures.

The inner part of the reef consists of huge branching elkhorn coral formations, big brain and other boulder corals, and platforms of ancient coral stone. Schools of blue tang swim

You can scuba dive at Loblolly Bay, but most people are content to leave tank and weights behind and enjoy the freedom of snorkeling. The coral comes to within tummy scratching distance of the surface and then drops down into a maze of caves, tunnels and gulleys.

Able to change its coloration to blend in perfectly with the sea floor, the peacock flounder is capable of disappearing in plain sight. This flat fish begins life upright until one eye slowly migrates over to join the other and the fish settles down to life on its side.

The largest of the cleaning shrimp, the banded coral shrimp works with two sets of clawed legs. This one is laden with eggs, which are clearly visible as a green mass attached to the shrimp's belly.

en masse, stopping as a group to nibble algae off the rocks. Sturdy gorgonians wave in the surge. Large stoplight parrotfish swim up to a piece of coral, bare their fused teeth and, with an audible crunch, bite off a chunk. The coral will be ground up in their gullets to extract the algae within. The parrotfish then excrete the processed coral as a silt cloud. This process results in a goodly amount of the fine sand beaches you've come all these miles to lie on.

The highlight to the reef structure are the deep holes and caves that cut through coral. There are sheer drops from just below the surface to the bottom at 30 feet (9 m). Various dead-end caves pockmark the reef. Several sand-floored tunnels pass right through. In the gloomy interior of these tunnels lurk a surprising amount of good-sized fishes. Big schoolmaster snappers, horse-eye jacks and groupers linger in the shadows. You can spend hours exploring these caves and the maze-like passages through the reef structure.

Caution. If the north swell is really up, Loblolly can be undivable. Even if you don't mind severe surge, in such conditions the sand will be so stirred up that visibility is reduced to a minimum. Likewise, all that water coming in over the top of the reef has to get out somewhere. There are currents running along shore and even some rip-like currents heading out to sea. The biggest hazard here is to be pushed up on the coral by the surge.

45. THE *PARAMATTA* (S)

DEPTH:	10-40 FEET
	(3-12 M)
LEVEL:	ADVANCED
ACCESS:	BOAT
ANCHORAGE:	NONE

One of the last of the great paddle-wheel steamers, the *Paramatta* ran up on Horse Shoe Reef on June 30, 1859. Iron-hulled and 330 feet (100 m) long, with a beam of 44 feet (13 m), she was owned by the Royal Mail Steam Packet Company, the same company which later (1865) built the 310-foot (94 m) propeller-powered RMS *Rhone*.

Unlike most ships driven up on a reef, the *Paramatta* did not immediately break up and take on water, but remained intact for a long time. Ships were dispatched from St. Thomas to salvage her, but to no avail. More importantly (as far as the RMS Packet Company was concerned), the other ships picked up the mail, passengers and cargo the *Paramatta* was carrying from Great Britain to St. Thomas and delivered it throughout the West Indies on schedule.

After a month of failed salvage attempts, and with hurricane season closing in, the crew was forced to abandon their ship. The local Anegadians continued to pick her clean of everything they could take, bolted down or not.

Today the *Paramatta*'s stern sits in 40 feet (12 m) of water and her bow, virtually flattened, in about 10 feet (3 m). The large chains and anchors that were used in futile attempts to pull her off the reef can be seen stretching seaward from the ship. The stern, with square portholes, sits in a valley created by huge elkhorn coral formations, magnificent giant sea fans and various boulder corals. Schools of blue tang, large parrotfishes and creole wrasse hover about the wreck and nearby reef.

Much of the wreck has been leveled over the years and the rest has been claimed by encrusting marine life. But the *Paramatta* does offer the opportunity to explore a rarely visited wreck and a piece of the Industrial Revolution, an ocean-crossing, iron-hulled paddle-wheel steamer. Not many dive guides know how to locate the wreck and, as it is on the exposed side of Horse Shoe Reef, conditions usually prevent it from being dived safely.

46. THE *ROCUS* (S)

DEPTH:	0-40 FEET
	(0-12 M)
LEVEL:	ADVANCED
ACCESS:	BOAT
ANCHORAGE:	NONE

The *Rocus*, also known as the Bone Wreck, sank in 1929. A steel 380-foot (115 m) Greek freighter, the *Rocus* was bound from Trinidad to Baltimore with a load of cattle bones to be

The coral crab is almost never seen by day when it hides in the deep recesses of the reef. At night, however, is can be seen foraging out in the open.

made into fertilizer when she struck the southern tip of Horse Shoe Reef. She now lies on her starboard side, with her stern in 40 feet (12 m) of water and her bow just below the surface. Until 1979, when hurricanes David and Frederick blew through, the bow of the *Rocus* projected about 12 feet (4 m) above the surface and was used as a navigational marker.

After more than 60 years underwater, the *Rocus* is largely broken up. The ocean floor is covered with cattle bones and wreckage. The engine, large boilers 20 feet (6 m) in diameter, and winches are still recognizable. Stacks of chain are attached to a massive anchor on the port bow. Huge sea fans and other hardy corals adorn the tortured wreckage. Stands of elkhorn coral are on the surrounding reef; delicate corals, such as staghorn, can be found in deeper water near the stern. Ocean triggerfish, black durgon and jacks abound. Nurse sharks and green moray eels can be found under ledges.

Standing on the bottom in 40 feet (12 m) of water, you get a view of the rounded stern, deck railings, davits and the ship's superstructure that extends upwards some 20 feet (6 m) or more. The ship's three-bladed propeller was removed by divers in the early 70's. But the aperture, where the mighty prop once turned, is a giant archway that you can swim through.

Caution. Conditions are usually very surgy and the wreck is often undivable because of the open ocean swells. There really is no way you can dive this wreck on your own. To find it and the route through the reef, you need to hire someone with extensive local knowledge and experience.

The *Rocus* is a fascinating, if not macabre (due to all the bones) wreck. The fish life and high relief of the ship make for good photo subjects. As it is not dived very often and is surrounded by a treacherous reef that has claimed hundreds of other vessels, you may feel a sense of adventure and discovery that is missing from a lot of other dives.

CHAPTER **VII**   JOST VAN DYKE

AT A GLANCE

Jost Van Dyke sits to the northwest of Tortola, a picturesque accent to the views from Cane Garden Bay and Sage Mountain. Named after a Dutch pirate, Jost Van Dyke rises steeply from the sea to a maximum elevation of 1,060 feet (321 m). The fourth largest island in the territory, JVD is roughly 4 by 1-1/2 miles (6.5x2.4 km) in size. With a small population of approximately 140 people and no major development, Jost Van Dyke remains largely unspoiled. Reliable electricity and modern phone service have only recently been initiated. Off the eastern tip of the island are the yachtsmen's playgrounds of Little Jost Van Dyke, Green Cay and Sandy Cay. These little islands are very popular with the day sail and yacht charter crowds. To the west lie Great Tobago and Little Tobago, the westernmost islands in the BVI.

EXPLORING JOST VAN DYKE

There are only three developed harbours on Jost Van Dyke, all on the south shore. White Bay is on the western end. Its exquisite white sand beach is protected by a series of reefs lying across the wide entrance to the bay. The beach is one of the finest in the BVI and because so few boats navigate through the reef, it's a fairly private and exclusive destination. The Soggy Dollar Bar boasts the "original" painkiller. There is fairly good snorkeling along the reef.

Just around the point to the east is Great Harbour, the largest settlement on the island. In addition to customs and immigration, there's a photogenic church and a slew of beach bars all built right along the sandy beach. The most famous is Foxy's Tamarind Bar and Restaurant, better known as just "Foxy's." Over the years it has become an institution for cruising sailors. Foxy Callwood, accompanying himself on the guitar, loves to sing Calypso ballads which he makes up as he goes along. When customers walk into his restaurant, Foxy often spontaneously creates songs about them. He is also the founder of the Jost Van Dyke Preservation Society, dedicated to protecting JVD's natural beauty. The annual Foxy's Wooden Boat Regatta has been hosted by Foxy and his wife Tessa for over 20 years. Their New Year's Eve parties are also legendary. People in the know say there are just three places to be on New Year's Eve: Paris, Times Square in New York City and Foxy's. Other barefoot beach bars include Ali Baba's, Rudy's, Happy Laury and Club Paradise.

Continuing east by boat or along the rough track that's carved into the coastline, the next bay is Little Harbour. Even less developed than Great Harbour, Little Harbour (sometimes called Garner Bay) still boasts several friendly beach bars, such as Harris' Place, Abe's, and Sidney's Peace and Love. With their uninhibited delight in the good times, these half dozen Jost Van Dyke bar-restaurants and their entrepreneur owners epitomize the Caribbean spirit: "Don't worry, be happy."

The fireworm, or bristleworm, is one of the few "touch-me-not" creatures on the reef. The white tufts in-between the branching gill filaments running along the sides of the worm are minute bristles. If disturbed the worm extends the bristles which can easily penetrate human skin, causing pain and itching. The fireworm feeds on soft corals. This worm has ingested several inches of a branch down its gullet.

The little islands lying off Jost Van Dyke offer some great diving and fantastic scenery. Sandy Cay and Sandy Spit (off Green Cay) are picture-perfect renditions of a tiny tropical paradise ringed by golden beaches, capped by tall swaying palm trees and surrounded by azure seas. In fact, you'll see them on plenty of postcards. Great Tobago to the west has been designated as a sanctuary for the magnificent frigatebird colony nesting there.

WHERE TO STAY

It doesn't make too much sense to stay on Jost Van Dyke if you plan on doing any scuba diving, as there are no dive facilities on the island. In fact, there isn't much in the way of accommodations other than White Bay Sandcastle, with four villas on the beach,

Foxy Callwood loves to entertain at his famous beach bar. In addition to singing spontaneous calypso ballads about guests, Foxy is also very active in the Jost Van Dyke Preservation Society, dedicated to preserving both the culture and unspoiled natural beauty of JVD.

Rudy's Mariner's Inn, Sandy Ground Estates and a couple of campgrounds.

EAT, DRINK AND BE MERRY

Yes, this is the thing to do on Jost Van Dyke. Many a visitor has spent a memorable afternoon and evening wandering from Abe's to Laury's and so on down the coast, sampling the rum drinks and cold beers.

WHAT TO DO

There's not much in the way of structured recreation here. Bar hopping, beachcombing, hiking and snorkeling are about it. Most visitors coming to Jost Van Dyke do so by yacht, so they are fairly self-sufficient when it comes to entertainment. The day-sail boats

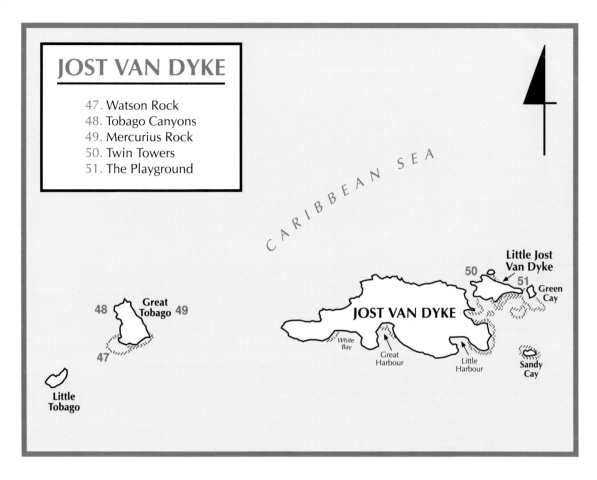

JOST VAN DYKE

CARIBBEAN SEA

Little Jost
Van Dyke

50

51

Green
Cay

Great
Tobago 49

48

JOST VAN DYKE

47

White
Bay

Great
Harbour

Little
Harbour

Sandy
Cay

Little
Tobago

Only in the eyes and fin edges is there a hint of blue in this juvenile blue tang. As the tang matures it will turn all blue. Most fishes change color as they mature; some species even change sex.

usually head straight to Sandy Cay or Sandy Spit, and spend the day sunning and snorkeling. If you want to get to Jost Van Dyke itself, a ferry leaves several times a day from West End, Tortola. The settlement at Great Harbour is worth a slow stroll and there is a trail that winds up the steep hills behind Little Harbour to a fantastic view. Foxy's has a gift shop and Ali Baba sells crafts. On Sandy Cay, which is still owned by the family, there is a narrow path encircling the island, providing a botanical tour of sorts.

DIVING AND DIVE SHOPS

Though there are no dive facilities on the island, both Baskin in the Sun (out of their West End shop) and Blue Water Divers dive Jost Van Dyke and its surrounding islands. While summertime is generally considered the best time to dive here, calm diveable days in the winter aren't that rare. Part of the joy of diving sites like Great Tobago and Watson Rock is that you'll be on the cutting edge. Even in the 1990's, when there aren't supposed to be any adventures left (especially in the Caribbean) you can explore underwater habitats that very few other people have seen.

DIVE SITES

Great Tobago

47. WATSON ROCK

DEPTH:	15-55 FEET
	(5-17 M)
LEVEL:	ADVANCED
ACCESS:	BOAT
ANCHORAGE:	NONE

Not found on many charts, Watson Rock is a tiny sentinel out in open ocean, between the lonely islands of Little and Great Tobago. While few people have heard of it, even fewer have dived it. The rock sits on the edge of an underwater shelf that extends from Great Tobago. Anchoring is difficult and should be done on the northwest side, in the lee of the rock.

At first glance it might appear that you can easily circumnavigate 89-foot-tall (27 m) Watson Rock on one dive, but as you wind in and out of the canyons, and perhaps fight a current, you'll find out why the local dive guides usually cover less ground.

Off the northwest side is a series of pinnacles, sheer slabs really, that stick up 20 to 40 feet (6-12 m) from the bottom at 55 feet (17 m). A long steep-walled canyon lies between them and Watson Rock. A little to the east is an encrusted archway at about 15 feet (5 m). If the waves are up, the surge in this shallow canyon can be dangerous. There are also a couple of small dead-end caves projecting back into the rock. The walls of all these overhangs and ceilings are covered with encrusting sponges and delicate corals, as well as banded coral shrimp, arrow crabs and juvenile angelfishes. Eagle rays are often seen here, as they are at most of the northside sites. Occasional turtles, nurse sharks and the regulars—parrotfishes, snappers, filefishes and barracudas—round out the menagerie.

Caution. Again, as with most of these outlying locations, we must advise that this is a very weather-dependent site and even under perfect conditions, it should be dived with professionals because of its extreme remoteness.

48. TOBAGO CANYONS

DEPTH:	35-100 FEET
	(11-30 M)
LEVEL:	ADVANCED
ACCESS:	BOAT
ANCHORAGE:	NONE

At the western limits of the BVI, on the far side of Great Tobago Island, are three dive sites.

The most intelligent of all invertebrates, the octopus is a cunning nighttime hunter. Deftly probing every crack and crevice of the reef with its eight sucker-laden tentacles, the octopus feeds mostly on crabs and mollusks, whose shells it often discards outside its den.

During the day cardinalfishes can be found hiding in the spines of sea urchins or in the recesses of caves. At night they emerge to forage on small invertebrates. The sheer wall behind this cardinalfish is the flank of a sleeping parrotfish.

The summit of Mercurius Rock lies hidden beneath the surface. Few divers know of its existence and even fewer know how to locate it.

49. MERCURIUS ROCK

DEPTH:	15-65 FEET
	(5-20 M)
LEVEL:	ADVANCED
ACCESS:	BOAT
ANCHORAGE:	NONE

Mercurius Rock is a submerged seamount pinnacle situated in the outer reaches of the British Virgin Islands less than one mile (1.6 km) east of Great Tobago. It is located between Great Tobago and Jost Van Dyke and is not often dived. In fact, it's not easy to find. Because it lies below the surface and there are no plans to put a NPT mooring in place, virtually the only way you can dive it is with a knowledgeable local dive guide.

The pinnacle comes to within 15 feet (5 m) of the surface. Actually there are three peaks that rise from the main formation. They drop off steeply to about 30 feet (9 m) and then the slope is more gentle. The flanks of Mercurius Rock are covered with deep-water gorgonians, sea fans, hard corals and waving fields of soft corals.

The highlight of the site is a long swim-through tunnel located at a depth of 30 feet (9 m) on the side of the biggest peak. The tunnel extends almost 100 feet (30 m). At 6 to 10 feet (2-3 m) across, it is big enough for divers to pass one another. The inside is filled with swirling schools of glassy sweepers, and slipper and spotted lobster, as well as shy groupers. The walls are adorned with brightly colored sponges and cup corals. The site also boasts another smaller tunnel.

Along the deeper south side of the rock at 55 to 60 feet (15-18 m) are a series of ledges. These host a community of lobsters, delicate invertebrate creatures and an occasional moray eel.

Caution. Due to its remoteness and exposure to the open ocean, this is considered an advanced dive and not for everyone. But if sea conditions and accessibility coincide, jump on board the dive boat and give one of the BVI's rarely visited dive sites a chance. Who knows, you may be one of the lucky ones to see dolphins.

The central one, Tobago Canyons, is located off a small cove on the west side of this remote island, just north of a little beach. From the shoreline the bottom slopes away to about 50 feet (15 m) and then drops a little steeper to the bottom at more than 100 feet (30 m). The slope is alive with corals and sea rods, and embellished with sponges and fans.

Just off the edge of the slope, a huge coral mound rises up from the depths to crest at 70 feet (21 m). This rounded hummock is a solid mass of hard corals. The top is all convoluted and pockmarked with small holes and crevices between the corals. There are fewer fishes here than on the main reef, though monster 10- and 12-foot (3-4 m) nurse sharks have been seen.

After exploring the hummock, swim back across the gap to the slope and work your way north (left facing shore). There are a couple of canyons cut back into the reef and even a few narrow walled cracks at about 35 feet (11 m). A couple of resident hawksbill turtles are regularly seen. Visibility here can vary from excellent to downright miserable.

Peering nervously from within the protective confines of a tube sponge, a tobaccofish checks to see whether it's safe to come out. Many fishes take shelter where they find it—in discarded cans, shipwrecks or even old boots.

A viral epidemic wiped out 99 percent of the spiny sea urchin population in the 1980's, but these animals are slowly making a comeback. Though they are often considered a nuisance by divers, they perform a vital role on the reef by grazing on algae that might otherwise overgrow living coral.

Little Jost Van Dyke

50. TWIN TOWERS

DEPTH:	40-90 FEET
	(12-27 M)
LEVEL:	ADVANCED
ACCESS:	BOAT
ANCHORAGE:	S. SIDE OF LITTLE
	JOST VAN DYKE

Tucked away behind a small point on the north side of Little Jost Van Dyke is another site boasting unusual topography. The "Twin Towers" of this site are two large monolithic rock formations rising from 90 feet (27 m).

From the rocky shoreline, the bottom drops straight down to 40 feet (12 m) and then continues as a slope down to a sandy bottom at 90 feet (27 m). Along this slope are other, smaller rock formations offering an abundance of tiny fish-filled grottos, mini-canyons and caves. Schools of reef squid are commonly seen here. They are fascinating to watch as they gently scull along with their lateral fins, often spread out in a line like a phalanx of guardsmen. Startle them and they're gone, jetting off with a squirt of ink and a blast of water out their siphons. Spotted eagle rays are also regular visitors, but divers are often too busy looking down at the reef and miss them as they silently soar by.

In springtime the fry can be so thick here that they darken the water. From a boat, they look like a moving shoal. Underwater, they'll completely engulf a diver, opening up to let the diver's exhaust bubbles thunder by and then close up again. The immensity of their numbers and synchronized movement can be mesmerizing, even overwhelming. That serene spell is easily shattered when a couple of large silver-plated tarpon rocket past, pursuing the fry.

At 90 feet (27 m) your bottom time is limited, but take advantage of your brief allotment to explore the base of the Twin Towers, especially the convoluted rock and rubble area between the two. Their sides are not overly covered with corals, but their colossal stature is impressive.

Caution. Like most north side sites, Twin Towers should not be attempted when the north swell is up.

51. THE PLAYGROUND

DEPTH:	15-70 FEET
	(5-21 M)
LEVEL:	INTERMEDIATE
ACCESS:	BOAT
ANCHORAGE:	GREEN CAY

From the calm sandy anchorages on the south side of Green Cay and nearby tranquil Sandy Spit, it is difficult to imagine that there is an exciting dive just on the other side of Green Cay. However, the narrow pass between Green Cay and Little Jost Van Dyke is too shallow (three feet) for anything but a dinghy or shallow draft dive boat. Most boats will have to circle all the way around Green Cay to the dive site mooring. It is tucked into a little cove on the northwest side of the island. The cove provides some measure of protection from the Atlantic, but if the swells are up, it would be prudent to choose another site. Also wind shifts can swing your boat 180 degrees and you could end up on the rocks.

Directly beneath the boat, the sea floor is completely covered with hard corals and gorgonians. Parrotfishes, squirrelfishes and occasional reef squid enjoy the calm here. As you head north around the point, look for a large formation of pillar coral in 25 to 30 feet (8-9 m) of water. Maintain this depth until you reach a series of huge boulder/pinnacles on the exposed north side. These make up the main attraction of the site. They are covered with marine growth: hard and soft corals, delicate branching hydroid fans, and brightly colored sponges. Overhangs are filled with fishes—sweepers, juvenile angelfishes, glassy minnows and fairy basslets. At the base of some of the boulders are little hollows and depressions formed between the boulder and the bedrock. Lots of marine life live in these protected areas. At 50 feet (15 m) there is a large swim-through you can explore. Two others are hidden in the rocks.

There is a concentration of piscine energy on this site. Schools of barracudas patrol the outskirts. Black margates and other grunts and snappers occupy the spaces between the rocks and skittishly slink away upon your bubbling approach. Turtles are often seen paddling between the pinnacles. Large dog snapper and individual jacks scour the reef searching for unwary prey. A school of horse-eye jacks hovers in the water column along with a stately eagle ray. Creole wrasse and bright porkfish add a splash of color.

You don't have to go deep to get a lot out of this site. In fact, if you stay shallow along the shoreline and continue past the huge boulders, you can sometimes see huge tarpon swim in the white foam where the waves break against the rocky shoreline. A good turn around point is a vertical chimney, big enough for one diver at a time, that goes up through the reef from 60 to 30 feet (18-9 m).

APPENDIX 1

EMERGENCY NUMBERS

VISAR	Channel 16
	999 (ask for Fire & Rescue)
	(Office) 494-4357
BVI Fire & Rescue	999
	(Office) 494-3473
Virgin Island Radio (St. Thomas)	Channel 16
	809- 776-8282
Tortola Radio	Channel 16
	494-4116
US Coast Guard (San Juan)	Channel 16
	787-729-6770
Peebles Hospital, Road Town	494-3497
Ambulance, Tortola	999
St. Thomas Hospital	809-776-8311
St. Thomas Recompression Chamber	
	809-776-2686
Saba Recompression Chamber	
	011-59-946-3295
Roosevelt Roads Recompression Chamber	
	787-865-4520
Divers Alert Network (DAN)	919-684-8111

Note: You should generally work through VISAR or the hospital for evacuation. Do not call the chambers directly.

Emergency Assistance—VISAR

If you are diving from your own or a chartered boat and need emergency assistance, contact the Virgin Island Search and Rescue (VISAR). This volunteer organization can provide rescue assistance, including helicopter and speedboat evacuation, medical attention, and hospital and recompression chamber readiness.

Emergency Communications Procedure

One person should be responsible for communications and stand by the radio until all arrangements have been made. Tune the VHF radio to Channel 16, press the microphone button, and clearly and calmly call "Mayday" three times. Then state the name of your boat, your location and the nature of the emergency. Pause for one minute before repeating your Mayday.

Virgin Islands Radio (marine operator in St. Thomas) or Tortola Radio (BVI marine operator) monitor Channel 16 and will connect you to VISAR. VISAR will coordinate rescue efforts.

You can call the agencies directly with a cellular phone, however, your Mayday will not be broadcast over the public VHF radio. So if you need immediate lifesaving efforts use the VHF radio, and perhaps a commercial dive boat or vacationing doctor may be nearby.

Recompression Chambers

There is no chamber in the BVI, but there are three in the region. One is at the hospital in St. Thomas, USVI; one is at Roosevelt Roads Navy Base in Puerto Rico (it is only available to the public when there are no Navy divers in the water); and one is on Saba, Netherlands Antilles. This one is available 24 hours a day, and immigration permits immediate access to the chamber during a diving emergency.

Divers Alert Network (DAN)

The Divers Alert Network (DAN), a non-profit membership organization affiliated with Duke University Medical Center, operates a 24-hour emergency number **(919) 684-8111** (emergencies only) to provide divers and physicians with medical advice on treating diving injuries. DAN can also organize air evacuation to a recompression chamber.

Since many emergency room physicians do not know how to properly treat diving injuries, it is highly recommended that in the event of an accident, you have the physician consult a DAN doctor specializing in diving medicine.

All DAN members receive $100,000 emergency medical evacuation assistance and a subscription to the dive safety magazine, *Alert Diver*. New members receive the DAN *Dive and Travel Medical Guide* and can buy up to $125,000 of dive accident insurance.

DAN offers emergency oxygen first-aid training, and provides funding and consulting for recompression chambers worldwide. They also conduct diving research at Duke University's F.G. Hall Hyperbaric Center.

DAN's address is 3100 Tower Blvd., Suite 1300, Durham, NC 27707. Their non-emergency medical information number is (919) 684-2948. To join call (800) 446-2671.

APPENDIX 2

Useful Numbers

Tourism Offices

United States
370 Lexington Ave., Suite 511
New York, NY 10017
212-696-0400   800-835-8530

1804 Union St.
San Francisco, CA 94123
415-775-0344   800-232-7770

United Kingdom
110 St. Martin's Lane
London WC2N 4DY
44-171-240-4259

Germany
Sophienstr. 4
D-65189 Weisbaden
49-611-300262

British Virgin Islands
Social Security Building
Waterfront Street, PO Box 134
Road Town, Tortola, BVI
809-494-3134

Car Rentals

Tortola
Airway Car Rentals	4-4502
Alphonso Car Rentals	4-3137
Anytime Car Rentals	4-2875
Avis	4-3322
Budget	4-2639
Caribbean Car Rental	4-2698
Denzil Clyne Jeep & Car Rental	5-4900
Hertz	5-4405
International Car Rentals	4-2516
National Car Rentals	4-3197

Virgin Gorda
Andy's Car Rentals	5-5511
Potter Gafford Car Rentals & Taxi	5-5329
Speedy's Car Rental	5-5240

Anegada
Anegada Reef	5-8002

Airlines

American Airlines	800-751-1747
American Eagle	5-2559
Fly BVI Charters	5-1747
Gorda Aero	5-2271
Liat	5-1187

Courier Services

DHL	4-4659
Federal Express	4-2297
Inland Messenger Service	4-6440
Rush It	4-4421

Calendar of Events

January
Hibiscus show
February
Sweethearts of the Caribbean Classic Yacht &
    Schooner Regatta
Easter Time
Virgin Gorda Easter Festival
Easter Monday Fishing Tournament
April
BVI Spring Regatta
June
Pursuit Sailing Race
"Hook In, Hold On" Wind Surfing Regatta
July
Territory Day
Start of Festival, Festival Village
August
August Monday; Festival Parade
Anegada Sailing Race
September
Foxy's Wooden Boat Regatta
October
Moorings Interline Regatta
Pro-Am Regatta
November
BVI Charter Boat Show
Around Tortola Sailing Race
December
Gustave Wilmerding Race

APPENDIX 3

[handwritten: Island Diver Ltd Capt. Read P.O. Box 3023 809-494-3878 Road Town Tortola BVI (R)]

DIVE CENTERS & LIVEABOARDS

Dive Centers

Aqua Ventures Scuba Services
Inner Harbour Marina
PO Box 852
Road Town, Tortola, BVI
800-698-6579
809-494-4320
Fax: 809-494-5608

Baskin in the Sun *[handwritten: Alan Baskin + Eva Cope]*
Prospect Reef Resort, Soper's Hole
PO Box 108
Road Town, Tortola, BVI
800-233-7938
809-494-2858 (Prospect Reef Resort)
809-495-4582 (Soper's Hole)
Fax: 809-494-5853

Blue Water Divers *[handwritten: Mike + Keith Royle]*
Nanny Cay Resort & Marina, Hodges Creek
Marina
PO Box 846 *[handwritten: Box 437]*
Road Town, Tortola, BVI *[handwritten: Rendezvous (R)]*
809-494-2847
Fax: 809-494-0198

Dive BVI *[handwritten: Joe Giacinto]*
Virgin Gorda Yacht Harbour, Leverick Bay,
Peter Island, Marina Cay
PO Box 1040 *[handwritten: (R)]*
Virgin Gorda, BVI *[handwritten: no air fills]*
800-848-7078
809-495-5513 (Virgin Gorda)
809-495-9705 (Peter Island)
Fax: 809-495-5347

Kilbrides Underwater Tours *[handwritten: Bert Kilbride]*
Bitter End
PO Box 46 *[handwritten: (R)]*
Virgin Gorda, BVI
800-932-4286
809-495-9638
Fax: 809-495-7549

Underwater Safaris *[handwritten: Bobs + Gail Stafford]*
Moorings-Mariner Inn, Cooper Island
PO Box 139 *[handwritten: (R)]*
Road Town, Tortola, BVI
800-537-7032

809-494-3235
Fax: 809-494-5322

Liveaboards

Cuan Law
105-foot (32 m) trimaran, 20 guests
Trimarine Boat Company
PO Box 362
Road Town, Tortola, BVI
800-648-3393
809-494-2490
Fax: 809-494-5774

Encore
53-foot (16 m) trimaran, 8 guests
PO Box 3069
Road Town, Tortola, BVI
809-776-6627

Gypsy Wind
46-foot (14 m) sloop, 2 guests
PO Box 3069
Road Town, Tortola, BVI
809-496-0448

Promenade
65-foot (20 m) trimaran, 10 guests
PO Box 3100
Road Town, Tortola, BVI
809-494-3853
Fax: 809-494-5577

Wanderlust
65-foot (20 m) trimaran, 16 guests
PO Box 5157
Charlotte Amalie, USVI 00803
800-724-5284
809-494-2405

Underwater Photography

Rainbow Visions Photography
Jim and Odile Scheiner
Prospect Reef Resort
PO Box 680
Road Town, Tortola, BVI
809-494-2749
Fax: 809-494-6390

INDEX

A **boldface** page number denotes a picture caption.
An underlined page number indicates detailed treatment.